The Stanford Album
A Photographic History,
1885-1945

THE

Margo Davis   Roxanne Nilan

STANFORD ALBUM

A Photographic History, 1885-1945

Stanford University Press

Stanford, California

1 9 8 9

Stanford University Press, Stanford, California
© 1989 by the Board of Trustees of the Leland Stanford Junior University
Printed in the United States of America
Photographic credits and CIP data appear at the end of the book
Published with the assistance of the Durfee Foundation

To Peter C. Allen

UNIVERSITY EDITOR EMERITUS

Preface

The Stanford University community is fortunate to have had, from its very founding, many alumni, faculty, and staff dedicated to documenting and preserving its
heritage. This dedication has given birth to a unique and rich photographic archive.
We have been inspired—Roxanne Nilan to write this text and Margo Davis to select
these photographs—by this extraordinary resource, and we would like to thank the
many colleagues and friends of the university who helped us complete *The Stanford
Album*.

As this three-year project has come to a close, we realize more than ever just how
collaborative the endeavor has been. When Roxanne Nilan came to the University
Archives in 1976, she found a photograph collection of prints and albums, scrapbooks and diaries, letters and ephemeral publications collected by her two predecessors, Ruth Scibird and Ralph Hansen. Much of her research and writing has
used these collections in combination with more traditional archival documents,
and as Curator of University Archives she has come to see these collections as providing a unifying heritage in an increasingly fragmented university community. To
make this heritage more available, she has written articles, given lectures, and developed exhibits, culminating in the history told in words and pictures in *The Stanford Album*. Thus, our special thanks not only to former curators Scibird and Hansen, but to our colleagues past and present who have helped the University Archives find and preserve the collective memory of the Stanford community.

Margo Davis, a photographer and teacher of photography, first joined the University Archives staff in 1985 to carry out a centennial project to make accessible its
voluminous photographic record. From this work sprang collaboration with Roxanne on the 1987 centennial exhibit "The Pioneer Years: Student Life at Stanford,
1891–1906." Margo's appreciation for the turn-of-the-century photographs was immediate and enthusiastic, and she had many ideas for presenting the images to a
wider public, including the original concept of *The Stanford Album* and its design as
a "family" photo album. She followed through on this vision by participating actively in the design process at Stanford University Press. Her special interest in the
history of photography inspired our introduction, which places Stanford's history
squarely within the evolution of the photographic medium.

Producing *The Stanford Album* has been a long, arduous, and much-loved project
that could not have been completed without a great deal of assistance. To the following, then, we offer our most heartfelt thanks.

Pete Allen, to whom this book is dedicated, is unparalleled in his knowledge of
Stanford. He has been an anchor of strength and support, the Delphic Oracle of the
Archives. Karen Bartholomew, good friend and source of editorial and historical
wisdom, devoted late nights and weekends to reading, commenting, correcting,
and listening, and threw us a life ring more than once. Mary Brown Lawrence has
volunteered hours of time and barrels of advice in preparing and organizing, finding, and filing photographs. Without her we would have drowned in a sea of images.

Robin Chandler and Linda Long of the University Archives helped chart our
search for all kinds of obscure images from prints and negatives to glass plates and
lantern slides. The staff of the Department of Special Collections and University Archives, and Paul H. Mosher, David C. Weber, and Leah Kaplan buoyed us with continued moral support.

Grant Barnes, Brigitte Carnochan, and Eugene Webb shared our optimism and were the first to set this project afloat. Ruth Levison Halprin, steadfast friend, contributed support both spiritual and financial. Her gift is in memory of her father, Robert Levison, whose fifty years of dedicated volunteering on behalf of Stanford made him unique in the history of the university. Anita Walker Scott's skill and knowledge kept us on a steady course toward final design and completion of the book.

The Durfee Foundation and the Stanford Historical Society offered vital financial support without which we would still be a long way from home port. In addition, we gratefully acknowledge the following contributors to the project: Helen and Peter Bing, Jill and John Friedenrich, Mel and Joan Lane, Linda and Tony Meier, Ernest J. Hilgard, and the "Quality of Life Fund" of the Office of the Dean of Student Affairs in memory of former deans of students.

And of course we must thank the many alumni—from the Pioneer Class forward—who made this book possible through the gift of their photographs and albums that have provided Stanford University with a visual memory of its formative years. We are also grateful to those alumni who graciously loaned us photographs and albums of the 1930's and 1940's, greatly enhancing the final two chapters.

Our apologies to those individuals who are unidentified by name in the legends that accompany the photographs. To a great extent, of course, this is because thousands of images have been left to us with little or no identification. But it is also because our intent in this album has been to give a glimpse of a community as a whole through a selection of images rather than to serve as a necessarily incomplete catalogue of community members.

Finally, a very special thank you must go to Jessamyn Nilan Axline, Julian Davis, Anika Davis, and James Axline, who endured our book-induced dementia and innumerable fast food dinners.

Margo Davis   Roxanne Nilan

Contents

Introduction

"From today painting is dead!"

These words—admittedly extravagant—were spoken by the French artist Paul Delaroche when photography was born 150 years ago. It was in August of 1839 that Louis Daguerre announced to the French Academy his invention of a process for transferring an image to a silvered metal plate. Two months later the earliest known surviving American daguerreotype was produced in Philadelphia.

It is a fitting coincidence that the art of photography has reached a milestone anniversary at the same time Stanford University is celebrating its Centennial Years (1985–91). The founders of the university, Jane Lathrop and Leland Stanford, sat for their wedding portraits in September 1850. These daguerreotypes, preserved in the Stanford University Archives, were just the beginning of the Stanfords' fascination for and patronage of the new art form. Not only did they carefully preserve the images of their family life, but Leland, early on in his business career, also perceived the value of the camera as a medium of documentation. This perception eventually resulted in a superb pictorial record of the planning, construction, and dedication of the university, some of which is reproduced in *The Stanford Album*.

Leland Stanford and Jane Lathrop posed for daguerreotype portraits in 1850, the year of their wedding.

A carte-de-visite of Jane Stanford in 1869, a year after the birth of her son in 1868.

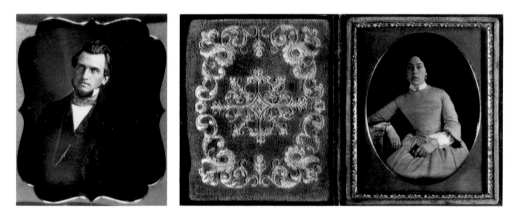

During the 1840's and 1850's the photographic process developed very rapidly. Henry Fox Talbot had patented his calotype, which had the tremendous advantage of providing a negative from which many prints could be made. In 1851, the wet-plate process was introduced, producing a negative on glass. Although the method was awkward, glass plates, like the calotype, could produce many paper prints. Cartes-de-visite, prints about the size of a calling card, became very popular.

It was also in the 1850's that Leland Stanford set out for the California gold fields. When he had secured his fortune—as a merchant, not a miner—he returned east to bring his wife to their new home in Sacramento. With their growing financial and social prominence, the Stanfords began to utilize the exciting new medium of photography. Members of the Stanford and Lathrop families were meticulous album keepers. Their portraits were taken at renowned studios—Taber of San Francisco, Alman of New York, and Sarony of Paris. Leland Jr. was photographed every year, posed in the Victorian setting of the photographer's studio. The Stanfords shared carte-de-visite prints and the slightly larger cabinet photographs with family and friends.

To capture the progress of the Central Pacific Railroad, of which he was president, Leland Stanford hired Alfred A. Hart to follow the construction crews from

The popular cabinet card was widely collected in family albums. Young Leland Stanford Jr. poses at the San Francisco studio of Bradley and Rulofson; the Stanford family sits for a portrait at the Walery Studio in Paris around 1881.

Eadweard Muybridge captures the family at home: Leland Jr., Jane Stanford, and Jane's sister Anna Maria Lathrop play billiards in their Sacramento home, 1874.

Leland Stanford stands in front of his store in the gold country of California in the early 1850's.

Stereograph card produced by Alfred A. Hart from his views of Central Pacific Railroad construction over the Sierra Nevada in the late 1860's.

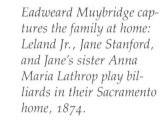

Sacramento across the Sierra Nevada to Promontory, Utah. Hart also photographed the Stanford Sacramento home. A few years later, Stanford hired the noted photographer Eadweard Muybridge to document first their remodeled Sacramento house, then their San Francisco Nob Hill home, keeping Muybridge in funds between his own artistic projects.

In 1872, Muybridge and Stanford began a collaboration on a photographic experiment that would prove Stanford's contention that, at one point in its fastest gait, a trotter has all four feet off the ground. This collaboration went on for nearly ten years. The results, which laid the foundation for the making of motion pictures,

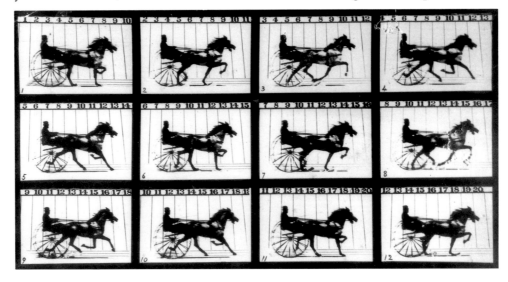

Trotter Abe Edgington was photographed at 1/1000 of a second in Eadweard Muybridge's horse-in-motion studies.

Detail of the cover of Leland Jr.'s "Cahier de Photographies" around 1880.

Carte-de-visite of Anna Maria Lathrop, photographed by her nephew Leland Jr.

Leland Stanford, Jr., Photo.   Menlo Park.

Archibald Treat's June 8, 1888, image of Inner Quad construction, looking to the smoke stack under construction behind the Quad.

were hailed internationally. The experiments provoked great controversy in the art world, changing dramatically the artistic representation of the horse in painting and sculpture. Stanford continued to document his trotters until his death in 1893, using the camera of local professional photographer and conservationist A. P. Hill to portray horses, employees, and Stock Farm facilities.

In keeping with his interest, Stanford hired Archibald Treat to photograph the construction of Leland Stanford Junior University between 1887 and 1891. Stanford, by then senator from California, was 3,000 miles away in Washington, D.C., much of this time, and the photographs proved invaluable to him, for he was inclined to pay close attention to minute details of construction.

Young Leland Jr. also became fascinated by photography, perhaps influenced by the extraordinary use of it by his father. His composition book was covered with a drawing of himself photographing under a dark cloth. This personal album was entitled "Cahiers de Photographies" and was filled with images that he made with his

Parisian wet-plate camera. He also had carte-de-visite mounts printed "Leland Stanford Jr., Photographer, Menlo Park." Into these mounts he placed the portraits he made of his aunt Anna Maria Lathrop and of his mother.

Leland Stanford Jr. was one of the rare amateurs of his day. Photography in the 1880's was still a cumbersome and expensive enterprise even though the decade did witness an end to the wet-plate process and the invention of the dry gelatin glass plate negative. By the late 1880's, the photographer was liberated finally from the need to have a darkroom on hand at the time of exposure. The era of carrying the darkroom into the field, onto the scene of battle, and into the Western wilderness

A. P. Hill's widely published photograph of President David Starr Jordan addressing the crowd at opening day, October 1, 1891.

At the 1904 faculty-senior baseball game, Professor William Dudley recorded Professor Charles D. Marx (far right) and friends.

A student photographer's camera case hangs from the limb of an oak as he takes a snapshot of two friends.

A motion picture camera is ready to capture an unknown event in Memorial Court around the time of the Great War.

had come to a close. The gelatin plate could be processed at any reasonable time after exposure. The innovation of gelatin films as well as of the hand camera revolutionized the art of photography, further making the medium practical for amateurs.

In 1888, George Eastman introduced one of the first Kodak cameras, sold ready-loaded with a roll of negative stripping paper film sufficient for 100 circular pictures 2½ inches in diameter. When the last exposure was made, the camera was packed and shipped to Eastman's factory where it was unloaded, charged with fresh film, and returned. "You push the button, we do the rest" was Kodak's advertising slogan. The world went shutter crazy.

The only images extant of opening day ceremonies at Stanford University in October 1891 were taken by photographers using a large-format glass plate. Nevertheless, the era of amateur photography with the small, informal, hand-held camera had clearly begun. It would have been possible for a matriculating Stanford student to photograph the October ceremonies with a hand-held Kodak camera.

A back porch along the row.

Cameras were expensive, though, and photography was most often limited by a "special occasion" mentality. The camera continued to evolve throughout the 1890's; in 1900 the popular Brownie camera was designed to be mass produced and sold at the amazingly low cost of $1.00. From the turn of the century, then, the "snapshot" image of campus life began to proliferate.

In the career of Berton Crandall, many of whose photographs are reproduced in this volume, we see both professional and amateur approaches reflecting Stanford photography of the time. Crandall was a student at Stanford during the earthquake era, graduating in 1907. During his student days, he began photographing around campus, and after graduation he opened a studio in Palo Alto. He photographed everything at Stanford—athletic events, drama productions, student parades, and many other campus rituals. He then made up proof albums so that people could visit his studio and order the photographic prints they wanted. Each proof print was carefully numbered and placed in an album for the year. Therefore, many of his photographs appear over and over in student albums of this period, 1904–36.

A page of the 1914 photo proof album of Palo Alto photographer Berton Crandall shows a variety of subjects: a Skull and Snakes Society initiation, a track team, Lagunita, and commencement.

Student albums reveal the more spontaneous life of the community: at Yosemite, 1936; a waterfight at Encina in the 1920's; in front of Roble Hall, 1938; Junior Day, around 1915; two friends at Stanford Stadium, 1945.

Like Crandall, students fortunate enough to own cameras intruded everywhere with the miraculous little box—into dormitories, dances, baseball games, picnics, and beer busts. The new camera encouraged people who had no previous experience to take up photography. The era of the snapshot now provided a glimpse into ordinary lives.

The Stanford Album draws heavily on the rich collection of student snapshots and photographic albums preserved in the University Archives. They reveal a unique view of informal campus life created by the students themselves—a kind of folk art. In contrast to the more studied formal portraits of athletic teams, social clubs, and academic processions—beautiful in their own way—we are privileged to glimpse in these albums very special spontaneous moments. The distinctive approaches of the photographers—both professional and amateur—enliven these pages. Of course, imperfections abound in the original prints—at times we have chosen to crop them for effect; at other times, we leave them, honoring these signs of age as reminders of the antiquity of the world we are picturing.

The world of the past, however, cannot be fully appreciated through the photographs alone. The text places the images in a cultural context that portrays the dynamics and character of each era. Stanford University evolved from a vision shared by two bereaved parents into a reality experienced by an entire university community. Text and photographs together weave the story of *The Stanford Album*.

This work comes at an important juncture in Stanford's history. Our purpose in compiling this album has been to revisit the Stanford community of old, leaving the post–World War II era for historians of the future. Our method has been to look through the magic of the camera lens, which permits this vanished world of college life to come alive again, to startle us and invite us to visualize the community that existed yesterday under the same arcades where we study, work, and meander today. We would like to pay a heartfelt tribute to that community, the Stanford community alive on the pages of this album—to the Stanfords themselves, who began the picture-taking, and to the students, faculty, and alumni, all of whom treasured their experience here so much that they not only *took* photographs but also *saved* them and *collected* them, in many cases returning them to the university to be preserved here for the many generations to follow.

It has several times been suggested to us that there was a limit to the beneficence of education, . . . but we have thought differently. We do not believe there can be superfluous education. As man cannot have too much health and intelligence, so he cannot be too highly educated.   LELAND STANFORD
Opening Day Address, October 1, 1891

Set among wild grainfields and paddocks, Leland Stanford Junior University was literally born on a farm. On the porch of his Palo Alto Farm home, Senator Leland Stanford put the finishing touches on a grant for the establishment of a university in the name of his dead son, Leland Jr.

The Palo Alto Farm was the centerpiece of Leland Stanford's landholdings scattered throughout Northern California. He began in 1876 with an initial purchase of 650 acres along San Francisquito Creek, about 30 miles south of San Francisco, and expanded the Farm to more than 8,800 acres of carefully laid out orchard, grain, and vegetable fields, a vineyard and winery, and grazing and stabling for his trotters and thoroughbreds.

At the heart of this favorite Stanford property was the Palo Alto Farm's trotting department, a vibrant complex of stables and paddocks, shops and tracks, employee housing and offices. More than a rich businessman's summer home, the Palo Alto Farm was a working ranch, a place of experimentation in the training and breeding of trotting horses. By the late 1880's, the Palo Alto Farm ranked with top Eastern horse breeding and training establishments as Stanford's horses competed nationally and broke world trotting records.

By this time, Stanford owned more than 100,000 acres in California, most of it used for experimental farming, stock breeding, and viticulture. But the Palo Alto Farm remained the family's favorite property and its home, second only to their residence in San Francisco.

The Farm was located between the thriving communities of Menlo Park and the smaller Mayfield. Like many of San Francisco's wealthy families, Leland and Jane Stanford were attracted to the area by its combination of rural atmosphere, climate, and convenience to their home in the City.

To the south lay the rich farm land of the Santa Clara Valley. Initially, the valley's economy, like that of San Francisco, centered on mining, lumbering, and some farming. Beginning in the 1880's, hundreds of small farms transformed the valley into miles of orchards, vineyards, vegetable farms, and nurseries.

The Palo Alto Farm bridged two geographic areas, the San Francisco peninsula and the valley, as well as two lifestyles: the wealth of the "polite society" building homes in Menlo Park mingled at this point with thousands of American and immigrant farmers and orchardists attracted to the remarkably productive soil of the "Valley of Heart's Delight."

A welcome change from the hectic business and political life surrounding Leland Stanford's career, the Palo Alto Farm also provided the Stanfords' only child, Leland Jr., with the rural atmosphere the Senator valued in his own upbringing. Active and healthy, young Leland thrived on the outdoor life of the ranch and spent much of his time hiking, riding, or working on construction of a miniature railroad line running from the house toward the stables.

Though Leland Jr. spent perhaps his happiest days on the Palo Alto Farm, he also greatly enjoyed traveling with his parents throughout Europe. Languages came easily to him, and he quickly learned French and German. During a stay in Belgium, Jane Stanford wrote of her twelve-year-old son, "Here everyone speaks French, so now he begins as naturally to use it as if he had always spoken it—he astonishes me."[1]

Forthright and businesslike, Leland Jr. was keenly interested in historical artifacts. As his parents visited studios and art salons and considered new acquisitions for their growing collection, Leland Jr. visited museums and historic sites. His excursions were more than random tours through exhibit halls; they often included interviews with museum directors and curators about their collections and profession, providing him with a practical introduction to museum management and scholarship. Especially interested in archaeology, Leland Jr. learned the rudiments of hieroglyphics from Georges Daressy, the Louvre's renowned Egyptologist, during an extended family visit to Paris in 1883. In Athens he was introduced to the Homeric scholar and archaeologist Heinrich Schliemann, whose excavations of the ancient city of Troy had stirred controversy and imaginations during the 1870's.

In 1883, the Stanfords leased a Fifth Avenue mansion in New York City in anticipation of Leland Jr.'s matriculation at Harvard. Leland Stanford Sr. became a patron of the Metropolitan Museum of Art, and the Stanfords became acquainted with Louis Palma di Cesnola, the Museum's director and an avid collector of Cyprian antiquities. At the end of the year, as the Stanfords headed to Europe, young Leland was armed with a letter of introduction from Cesnola to Sir

Philip Cunliffe Owens, director of the South Kensington Museum (now the Victoria and Albert Museum).

In the arts, the Stanfords seemed attracted to men of strong personality as well as talent. From Eadweard Muybridge, the eccentric photographer of Western landscapes, to Louis Meissonier, Parisian society leader and portrait painter, from the flamboyant Cesnola to the charismatic Schliemann, the Stanfords gravitated toward the outspoken and controversial, without sacrificing their insistence on value for dollar.

In addition to introducing their son to museums, directors, collectors, and archaeologists in the field, the Stanfords encouraged him to collect artifacts for his own small museum, housed on the upper floor of their San Francisco residence. He focused increasingly on antiquities as his taste matured, building the collection with small, strictly-accounted-for sums from his parents as well as from hunts for souvenirs at historic sites and gifts from Schliemann and other collectors.

In the spring of 1884, on a side trip to the excavations at Troy following his visit with Schliemann, Leland Stanford Jr. contracted what would later be diagnosed as a mild case of typhoid fever. After three weeks of recuperation in Florence, Italy, the crisis seemed passed, but suffering a relapse, he died late in the evening of May 13, 1884, just two months short of his sixteenth birthday. Sensational accounts appeared in American newspapers throughout 1884 and 1885 about Leland and Jane Stanford's grief at the death of their only child, and the Stanfords received a flood of sympathy letters and scores of unsolicited memorial poems. Irked at the media attention, Leland Stanford issued a statement to the press discounting the rumors of their abnormal grief and suggesting that behind them lay greedy men interested in one day challenging the Stanford will and their bequests to philanthropic projects.[2]

In fact, the Stanfords only dabbled in the popular Victorian mourning rituals of spiritualism and inspirational Christian literature. They found it far more satisfying to express their sadness through practical means. In many interviews, Leland Stanford credited their humanitarian work to his dream the night of his son's death in which Leland Jr. encouraged his father to "live for humanity." Years later, Jane Stanford recounted her husband saying, "How I wish I could remember all that he said to me in that dream. I know I resolved from that moment to build the university, and we both from that night resolved on this."[3]

Before returning to California in the late spring of 1884, they set in motion plans for several projects they envisioned establishing in the boy's name. They interviewed key men in education, art, and archaeology, and remained flexible regarding a combination of plans for a college or university at Palo Alto and a museum in San Francisco. Their plans would reflect not only their son's interests, but their own personalities, ideals, and ambitions formulated in their childhoods and developed through their years in California.

Leland Stanford, the son of an upstate New York innkeeper, farmer, and entrepreneur, had studied to be a lawyer in Albany, New York, after attending the Clinton Liberal Institute and the coeducational Cazenovia Seminary in upstate New York. Following a successful but brief practice of law in the Wisconsin boomtown of Port Washington, he joined his enterprising brothers selling mining supplies in the gold fields of California in 1852.

Selling supplies across a makeshift counter, Stanford found himself untrained and unprepared as a businessman. Yet hard work, practicality, and an eye for the potential investment guided him to a highly successful career in the gold fields, then as a merchant in Sacramento, and, ultimately, as senior officer of the most powerful transportation network in the West, the Central Pacific Railway and the Southern Pacific Company.

Typical of the merchant princes of the western United States, Stanford credited personal values of industry, ambition, character, good judgment, enterprise, and knowing the value of money rather than any advantage of social rank or classical education for his success. These values would become the foundation of the university he would envision.

By the 1880's, Stanford was recognized as a philanthropist and, as governor during the Civil War and a staunch supporter of Lincoln, had been credited with keeping a divided California in the Union. Stanford had a relatively positive image in the eyes of the California public in spite of his position as president of the politically powerful Central Pacific and Southern Pacific. His business partner, railroad vice president Collis P. Huntington, resented Stanford's popular image. When Stanford's interest in political office reawakened early in 1885, Huntington was vocal in his cynicism about the ignorant voting public and corrupt public officials alike. The rift between the two men became irreconcilable when Stanford won one of California's senate seats later that year, backed by a movement that drew a distinction between the man who ran the railroad and his opponent, Aaron Sargent, a man owned by the railroad and by Huntington. Stanford's candidacy also clearly was aided by early news of his plans for a new California university. Huntington, in turn, ridiculed the use of a railroad fortune on something other than railroad reinvestment and joked of the university project as "Stanford's circus." Years later, Huntington's attitude would jeopardize the university's financial security.

Like her husband, Jane Lathrop Stanford approached every task with seriousness and firm opinions. Thrifty and pragmatic in domestic affairs, she looked back with special fondness on the first years spent with her husband in California when, in order to save money for business investments, they made their own furnishings and she became quite a good carpenter.

Mrs. Stanford's sense of duty and her pride in family pervaded her role as hostess in San Francisco and

Washington, D.C. Following his early business success in California, Leland Stanford had suggested to his wife that they return to her parents' home of Albany, New York. Mrs. Stanford preferred California and remained one of its strongest boosters. At their Washington parties, a cornucopia of California would be offered to Eastern guests: meals featured fresh fruits and vegetables from the Stanfords' California farms and wines from their wineries at Palo Alto and Vina.

Jane Stanford's special philanthropic interest was the education and care of children. The first kindergarten in the West had appeared in 1878 and by the early 1880's Mrs. Stanford was an eager supporter. In 1885, she funded the establishment of five kindergartens in San Francisco under the auspices of the Golden Gate Kindergarten Association, and as honorary president she encouraged other society women to become actively involved. Other schools would soon follow—a free kindergarten in Mayfield, a school for the children of Palo Alto Farm employees and a night school for the adults, and a child care center for children of working women in Albany.

Following their son's death, the Stanfords continued to develop their contacts in the art and museum worlds and to build their collection of fine art as well as of the antiquities that would have captivated Leland Jr. An art museum became a major element of their plans. Mrs. Stanford in particular was determined to found a museum in her son's name, separate from the university project. The museum, finally established on the campus, would house a wide range of collections but would focus on Leland Jr.'s preference for Egyptian, Roman, and Greek antiquities. For the remainder of her life, Mrs. Stanford took an active

role in the development of the museum's collections and served as its director in all but name, joining a handful of wealthy women in the United States who were developing and promoting some of America's most significant private and public museum collections.

After taking office in March 1885, newly elected Senator Stanford spent only a few months in Washington, D.C., using much of his time in the East talking with leaders in American higher education. Unfortunately, few records remain of conversations with the university presidents he and Mrs. Stanford consulted. Memoirs of these men published many years later and contemporary newspaper accounts reveal that Stanford went about the business of planning his university in much the same way as he pursued his other activities: he solicited advice from men highly respected in the field. Charles W. Eliot of Harvard later recounted his interaction with the couple:

One impression left on my mind at the time was that Mr. Stanford really had two objects in view. He wanted to build a monument to his dead boy; but he also wanted to do something which would interest his wife for the rest of her life and give her solid satisfaction. . . . I thought, too, that she had done more thinking on the project than he had. . . . Altogether it was a very interesting interview.[4]

Eliot encouraged their plan to establish a university in California. Asked by Mrs. Stanford to estimate the cost of such a project in addition to land and buildings, he replied that a university charging no tuition ought to be endowed with at least five million dollars. "A silence followed," remembered Eliot, "and Mrs. Stanford looked grave; but after an appreciable interval Mr. Stanford said with a smile, 'Well, Jane, we could manage that, couldn't we?' And Mrs. Stanford

nodded."[5] The Stanfords ultimately would endow Leland Stanford Junior University with more than $20 million, four times the size of the Harvard University endowment.

Leland Stanford was profoundly influenced by two leaders in the movement toward a new American university: Eliot of Harvard and Andrew White of Cornell. In an era of extraordinary growth, vitality, and experimentation in education, White and Eliot were leading the university curriculum away from classical education for the leisured upper class toward a practical, career-oriented education for the American middle class.

With other educational reformers, White and Eliot sought to transform the American college from a receptacle of knowledge into a generator of knowledge, a "university." They looked to the German university model. There faculty were encouraged to conduct research as well as to teach, to produce new knowledge and new questions. They were joined in research by graduate students earning the new, advanced "doctoral" degree. Thus at recently opened Cornell University, at the 249-year-old Harvard, and at a handful of other institutions, the definition of learning was undergoing a major transition. Leland Stanford had little interest in the small Eastern liberal arts colleges; his Western institution would begin as a university.

Stanford was greatly impressed by White's work at Cornell. Since 1868, the Yale-educated White had guided Cornell University as a nondenominational institution dedicated to producing students equipped to take part in an industrial society. He wrote and spoke passionately on the potential of higher education.

Eliot shared White's belief in the utility of education and added a commitment to democracy, individual autonomy, and experimentation. His reforms at Harvard during the 1880's were considered by many to be subversive of college traditions, for he pressed for an open curriculum based on the "elective" system in which students could sample and select for themselves courses in a variety of disciplines.

By November 1885, twenty months after Leland Jr.'s death, the Stanfords' plans were in place. In a relatively quiet ceremony at their San Francisco residence, 24 trustees were enlisted to watch over the newly founded Leland Stanford Junior University. They were presented with an artistically calligraphed parchment, the "Grant of Endowment," which provided for the university's financial support, defined its scope and organization, named its trustees and formulated their duties. However, the Stanfords reserved the right to exercise all the powers and functions of the trustees until their deaths. The Board of Trustees was made up of Stanford's friends and business associates, among them some of California's most successful businessmen and a number of progressive lawmakers as well as railroad associates. They were practical, successful men. Only one had experience with the administration of a university—Horace Davis, former president of the University of California.

Emphasizing progress and practicality rather than classical tradition, the simply worded grant outlined a university that was purposefully utilitarian, nonsectarian, democratic, and coeducational, avoiding the "educational millinery" Leland Stanford found in many older universities.

Leland Stanford Junior University would be open to all students regardless of social position or sex; no tuition would be charged. It would train young people, male and female, for genuine careers in society rather than in ways to occupy their leisure time. The Grant of Endowment articulates great faith in American democratic government, individualism, and the work ethic. Woven throughout the grant is an underlying assumption that through education the American public would better govern itself and better respect the fruit of its labor.

Reaction in California to the founding of a new private university was mixed. Newspapers, divided politically between anti- and pro-railroad, reported this new Stanford project as it suited their readerships. The pro-railroad *Overland Monthly* said in December 1885, "Mr. Stanford was largely, take it all in all, the foremost citizen of the State; but by the completion of the present endowment he will become so to an extent that it is almost impossible to find paralleled in modern times." Other newspapers denounced the founding as a vengeful personal attack by Stanford on the University of California in order to appropriate the limited number of students on the West Coast qualified to attend a university. Some said it was a ploy by the Southern Pacific management to divert public attention from its monopolistic aggressions and political manipulations.

Comment in Eastern newspapers was more detached, though not necessarily less skeptical. The *New York Commercial Advertiser* remarked:

It is announced that Senator Stanford has made a will leaving 20 million dollars to the "University" which he has established in California. We hope that the statement is untrue . . . to attempt to create a great university Aladdin-like out of nothing but money is as useless as would be the building of a great summer hotel in Central Africa or an institution for the relief of destitute ship captains in the mountains of Switzerland. At present, Stanford's great wealth can only be used to erect an empty shell and to commemorate a rich man's folly.[6]

Many saw opportunity of their own. Letters poured in—requests for employment, offers of specialized equipment for sale, recommendations for students. Some offered their personal philosophy of education; others requested donations to their own education projects in other parts of the state. Some simply wrote their thanks.

The Stanfords seemed to ignore the public debate. Nor is there any evidence that they took seriously recommendations that they contribute to an established college or university rather than continue with plans for building a memorial institution in California. Leland Stanford was attracted, rather, to special characteristics of several of the universities he had visited—Cornell, M.I.T., Harvard, and Johns Hopkins.

Stanford assumed that as founder of a university, he could do no more than give it sustenance and a general direction toward practicality, efficiency, and social responsibility. "Extensive and expensive buildings do not make a university," he wrote. "It depends for its success rather upon the character and attainments of its faculty."[7] The university charter in place, he focused his attention on the men who could help him put the university into action and remained alert to the need to hire a strong president who would in turn select the faculty and student body.

During a visit to the Massachusetts Institute of Technology, Stanford was greatly impressed with the character and achievements of its president, Francis A. Walker. Stanford concluded that this was the type of leader he wanted to head his university and offered Walker the position. Walker declined but agreed to advise the Senator on an academic plan and visited the Palo Alto Farm in 1886. Acting on Walker's recommendations, Stanford hired the eminent Boston landscape architect Frederick Law Olmsted and the Boston architectural firm of Shepley, Rutan, and Coolidge.

Stanford's association with Olmsted was as trying as it was productive. Attracted to the setting of oak-studded hills on the 8,800-acre ranch, Olmsted was as interested in the site as in the pragmatic, democratic mission of the university described by Stanford. Olmsted envisioned an informal grouping of buildings in a park-like setting typical of his earlier college commissions. However, Stanford insisted on a large, formal space suitable to a memorial, and a site on level ground. Olmsted acquiesced with a striking quadrangle arrangement laid out in the grainfields with additional quadrangles planned for two sides.

With the site selected, the two men again disagreed, this time over the orientation of the quadrangle and the roads leading to it from the county road (El Camino Real). Olmsted specified two diagonal roads emanating from the central quadrangle, one leading to the town of Menlo Park, the other to Mayfield.

Stanford disagreed and called for a grand avenue leading from a train station in the newly conceived residential site of "University Park" (later Palo Alto) to the central quadrangle. Olmsted provided that grand avenue, with a long vista up "University Avenue" (now Palm Drive). At its end would be a dramatic opening at an oval of plantings to a sweeping panorama of low quadrangle buildings.

Landscaping remained natural, bowing to the arid nature of the countryside. The arboretum taking shape on a site near the planned quadrangle especially intrigued Olmsted. He saw in it an experimental nursery for his own uses throughout the West. But Olmsted grew impatient with the continuing struggle with Senator Stanford over ultimate control over the site and the project in general. The relationship slowly dissolved by 1890.

Stanford had a tense but highly productive relationship with architect Charles Allerton Coolidge as the architect designed the buildings to fit Olmsted's quadrangle plan. Living on-site in temporary quarters in the brick tower house at the Farm's "Running Ranch," the 28-year-old Coolidge, a younger and more patient man than Olmsted, sought to bring to life Stanford's ideas for a campus typical of California in color and at-

mosphere. During early design meetings with Olmsted and Walker, Stanford apparently suggested an architectural style reminiscent of the California missions, including the use of long arcades. The Romanesque style typical of the work of Shepley, Rutan, and Coolidge, inherited from their mentor, Henry Hobson Richardson, was easily compatible with Stanford's concept.

From groundbreaking in 1887 it took another four years to build the initial university buildings. Construction was delayed by a variety of causes. Olmsted and Coolidge found themselves overruled by managers from the Stanford estate, and communication with Senator Stanford, more than 3,000 miles away in Washington, D.C., was difficult. Much of the original plan would never be carried out.

The doubts and ridicule of the public became stronger as year after year passed and the university did not open. Finally, in March 1891, the buildings of the inner quadrangle were complete—except for a space left vacant for a majestic church structure—and two dormitories were under construction. Determined not to let another year go by, Stanford was faced with completing the next vital step: he needed a university president and a faculty, not to mention a student body.

Stanford had been searching for a president since 1885 when he had offered the position to Walker. By 1889, he had commented to a reporter, "The man I want is hard to find. I want a man of good business and executive ability as well as a scholar. The scholars are plentiful enough, but the executive ability is scarce. . . . If I cannot combine these two qualifications I will get a business man, or I will take the presidency myself."[8]

Stanford now approached Andrew White at Ithaca. White, looking forward to a well-earned retirement from Cornell, declined the presidency but recommended a Cornell protégé, the 40-year-old president of Indiana University, David Starr Jordan.

When Senator and Mrs. Stanford arrived in Bloomington by rail in "Car Stanford," Jordan was out of town delivering an impassioned speech on the value of publicly supported higher education. On his return the next day he found the Stanfords waiting for him.

Senator Stanford and Jordan discussed their educational philosophy and Stanford's ambitions for the California university.

Each man was impressed with the other. They shared not only a rural upper New York State upbringing, but firm beliefs in individualism, the importance of practical education, and the opportunity of upward mobility. Stanford offered Jordan the presidency of the new university with the lucrative salary of $10,000 a year—nearly three times his Indiana salary—for life. "After a short consultation with Mrs. Jordan, I decided with some enthusiasm to accept Mr. Stanford's offer, in spite of two apparent risks," Jordan later recalled in his autobiography. "As to the first, California was the most individualistic of the States and still rife with discordant elements. Secondly, the new institution was to be 'personally conducted,' its sole trustee a business man who was, moreover, active in political life. But the possibilities were so challenging to one of my temperament that I could not decline."[9] On his return to California, Stanford explained:

A thing that I feel very well satisfied about is the selection of David Starr Jordan as President of the University. . . . I consulted with President Andrew D. White of Cornell and with President Gilman of Johns Hopkins, and both of them testified to the ability and excellent qualifications of Professor Jordan. I might have found a more famous educator, but I desired a comparatively young man who would grow up with the University. . . . My interview with President Jordan was so satisfactory that I at once tendered him the position.[10]

Jordan's first task was to assemble a faculty. This was an especially frustrating experience even though the salaries offered were above average—and had to be, because of the university's location far from the center of American academic life and from other research facilities. Early in the summer of 1891, Jordan wrote in exasperation from Harvard, "I am off on a hunt for professors, but find my best hunting grounds about Cornell. In the Back Bay, where I am now, are men whom nothing would induce to go west of Springfield, and men whose regret of their lives is that they were born outside of Boston."[11]

Like Senator Stanford, Jordan turned his search to young men and women of promise who would grow with the university and build its reputation as they established their own. In the end, the majority of the first faculty was hired away from Cornell and Indiana universities, and Leland Stanford Junior University would be launched by the press as "The Cornell of the West."

Jordan brought to the task an infectious optimism. As the summer approached its end, he wrote to his friend and first faculty appointment, geologist John Casper Branner: "Nothing could be more promising than the present outlook here, and no place in the universe more delightful than Palo Alto. . . . When the students and faculty get here, the work of managing the institution will perhaps be more difficult."[12]

Ocean fog rolls over Palo Alto Farm foothills graced by coast live and valley oaks.

Archibald Treat's 1886 photographs, taken for campus planner Frederick Law Olmsted, captured topographical data from the hills overlooking the Farm down to Peter Coutts's farm buildings and, in the distance, the town of Mayfield.

Vestiges linger from Peter Coutts's Ayrshire Farm, purchased by Leland Stanford in 1882: Coutts's library with brick tower, his playful bridge, and the crenellated boundary tower on Mr. Page's mill road still exist, but the brick-lined lake is gone.

The saloons of nearby Mayfield may have irritated the
Stanfords, but that did not
discourage Jane Stanford
from endowing a free kin-
dergarten there: Miss Lily
Ransom and her charges,
April 1887.

The Palo Alto Farm took its
name from the landmark
that guided Spanish explor-
ers, an exceptionally tall
redwood, El Palo Alto.
Years later, the town of Palo
Alto did the same.

In 1888, Mrs. W. H. Myrick, wife of the photographer, sits with a friend beside the Farm reservoir, later named Lagunita, or "Little Lake."

Palo Alto drivers guide trotters around the mile-long training track near the paddocks.

Farm employees return from work in the foothills.

19

Overview of paddocks and key buildings of the Stock Farm's trotting department, one of the largest in the United States.

Brood mares were carefully selected for Leland Stanford's progressive breeding program.

The great Electioneer, purchased against the advice of Eastern experts, sired nine of the Farm's thirteen world champions.

Vina Belle, one of 166 Stanford trotters able to trot the mile in 2:30 or better.

22

Some of the Farm's 150 employees take time out for lunch.

Trotting department living quarters included the farmhouse and barn of previous owner D. Hoag, purchased by Stanford in 1876.

Eadweard Muybridge's 24-camera setup for the horse-in-motion experiments near the one-mile track.

Coachman Charles Wooster, with matched team of grays "Tom" and "Jerry," often drove the Senator along the eucalyptus-lined Governor's Avenue from the house to the barns and paddocks.

Through the Paddocks.

Leland Stanford entertained President Rutherford B. Hayes and his party at the Palo Alto home in 1880 while Mrs. Stanford and Leland Jr. were in Europe. The house was substantially remodeled in 1888 with the help of campus architects.

Thirty-nine-year-old Jane Stanford proudly holds her three-month-old son and only child. These are but a few of the many photos of Leland Jr: at two years, not quite four, (opposite) with his mother at six, and as a self-confident eight-year-old.

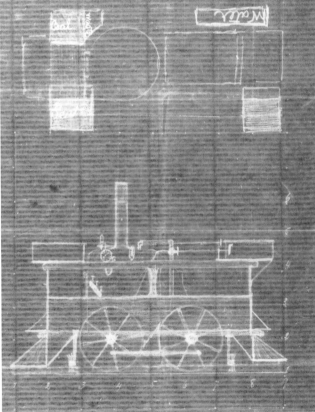

Active and robustly healthy, Leland Jr. loved things mechanical, recording his ideas in a sketch book and building a miniature railroad on the Palo Alto Farm, but he dreamed of becoming an archaeologist.

Leland Stanford Jr., Paris, 1883, a few months before his untimely death from typhoid fever.

In a quiet ceremony in the library of their San Francisco residence, Jane and Leland Stanford created a new California university in memory of their son.

GRANT

Founding and Endowing

THE LELAND STANFORD JUNIOR UNIVERSITY

After months of planning, the university's cornerstone was laid on May 14, 1887, the nineteenth anniversary of Leland Jr.'s birth, with speeches and a Menlo Park church choir. Afterward, architect Charles Coolidge kept drawing far into the night to stay one step ahead of the construction crew.

The solitary cornerstone sits amid the commotion of Inner Quad construction.

Archibald Treat's photo-graphs kept Leland Stanford informed of progress on the Quad while the Senator was away in Washington, D.C.

The arcades of the Inner Quad take shape, as does the men's dormitory, Encina Hall, patterned after a favorite Swiss hotel.

Leland Stanford decided to pave the Inner Quad with asphalt rather than the suggested paving blocks in order to speed up Quad completion by 1891.

Sphinxes adorning the new Stanford Mausoleum in the arboretum were deemed too feminine by Mrs. Stanford and were removed to the back.

A Southern Pacific spur line at Bonair Siding brought sandstone from its quarry near New Almaden to the Inner Quad where stonemasons carved on site.

This spot, reserved for Memorial Church, was not filled until 1903.

As work on Encina Hall
neared completion, the first
ten clapboard houses for
faculty families were
quickly built at a diagonal
along Alvarado Row.

Jane and Leland Stanford envisioned a progressive, tuition-free university offering a practical education to both men and women.

"The possibilities were so challenging to one of my temperament that I could not decline." David Starr Jordan, first president of Stanford University, 1891.

38

Ours is the youngest of the universities, but it is heir to the wisdom of all the ages, and with this inheritance it has the promise of a rapid and sturdy growth.   DAVID STARR JORDAN
Opening Day Address, October 1, 1891

On a hot afternoon in the summer of 1891, three tired faculty families stepped off the train at the Menlo Park station. Their leader was David Starr Jordan, president of the new Leland Stanford Junior University, or, as the public quickly dubbed it, "L.S.J.U." During the ten-day journey from upstate New York, the charismatic Jordan had painted a picture of elegant quadrangles, arcades in cool California sandstone, and vibrant halls of learning. Gathered into a waiting wagon, the group was driven to the Stanford family's ranch, an instant university campus.

One member of the group, Ellen Coit Elliott, later wrote of her first impression as they rode up Palm Drive:

Beyond was the winery, a grove of thickly foliaged oaks, a sunny open space with the Museum going up. Then, at a dramatic gesture from Dr. Jordan, we looked toward the foothills and saw The University, our goal, our destiny. . . . My heart sank. I had expected the University to be beautiful, imposing, adequate to high thoughts and noble purposes; and what I saw, some distance across a dry, dun waste, was a low, bare line of buildings, plain and stiff. . . . They appeared to me exactly like a factory.[1]

Jordan's idealism and Leland Stanford's ambitions for the university aside, Mrs. Elliott was correct in seeing that Leland Stanford Junior University was a half-finished complex of classrooms built in the open

fields, with inadequate housing, inconvenient community services, and a young and comparatively inexperienced faculty. It was hot and dusty and isolated from American academic life and urban amenities alike.

Yet within the next twelve years, those who joined together as students and faculty wove into place a community identity based on shared experiences, commonly held assumptions about college life, local legend, and local personalities. The very act of coming together to create this community would be enshrined in the university's history as its remarkable and exciting "pioneer years."

Stanford's first registrar and university historian, Orrin Leslie Elliott, ventured first to call it Stanford's "heroic age," an age of farsighted and generous founders, of courage in the face of financial crises, of inspiring leadership by its first president. Above all, Elliott pointed to "the loyalties and the light-heartedness and joyousness which characterized the life of the community, students and faculty, whatever the day might bring forth."[2]

At opening day ceremonies in the Quadrangle, October 1, 1891, Leland Stanford told the assembled students and some 1,500 visitors seated under a hot Indian summer sun:

It is our hope that the young women and the young men who graduate from Palo Alto shall not only be scholars, but shall have a sound practical idea of commonplace, everyday matters, a self-reliance that will fit them, in case of emergency, to earn their own livelihood in a humble as well as an exalted sphere. Added to this we wish them to go out into the world with a lofty sense of man's and woman's responsi-

bilities on earth in accordance with the highest teachings of morality and religion. . . . You, students, are the most important factor in the university. . . . All that we can do for you is to place the opportunities within your reach. Remember that life is, above all, practical; that you are here to fit yourselves for a useful career; also, that learning should not only make you wise in the arts and sciences, but should fully develop your moral and religious natures.[3]

Stanford University's much publicized intention to provide tuition-free, practical education in a fully co-educational setting, backed by the significant personal wealth of its founders, attracted far more students than anyone expected. The university administration anticipated some 250 young men and women would register; the fall quarter saw 555 students. All who qualified by credential or exam were admitted, including 255 freshmen of the "Pioneer Class of '95," 116 upperclassmen transfers from 25 different colleges, 37 graduate students, and 147 "special" students. Many had been personally encouraged to try college by Jordan during a summer speaking tour throughout the state.

This surprisingly large student body was continually compared to the 520 students enrolled at the older and more academically stable University of California. Critics attacked the wide-open enrollment that admitted 25 percent of its student body as "special." They hinted that Stanford's ranks were filled with those who did not pass the entrance requirements of the University of California. Registrar Elliott defended the large number of "specials," pointing to the university's commitment to provide an educational opportunity to the less privileged. The category was aimed at older, working-class male students (with a minimum age of twenty) who had not had the opportunity to attend qualified high schools or preparatory schools, but who wished to follow a course of study. Elliott predicted that those special students unqualified for college life would soon drop out while those with talent and ambition would qualify for regular student standing. This proved true, as one-third quickly made up academic deficiencies and were admitted to a degree-granting program.

After passing the entrance examination, administered at various sites up and down the coast by the tireless Elliott and a handful of faculty, the newly arrived Stanford student registered and paid a nominal fee. Selecting a faculty member or "major professor" to be his or her advisor and mentor, the student took courses to fill the faculty member's departmental requirements.

Jordan had introduced the major-professor system at Indiana University in the mid-1880's, although the selection there was made in the third year. Jordan shifted the choice to the first year, agreeing with Leland Stanford that each student must develop educational and career goals early. He acknowledged the student's ability, as well as responsibility, to select his or her course of study with the assistance of an influential faculty member. "Any pre-arranged course of study," Jordan declared, "is an affront to the mind of the real student."[4]

The major-professor system also assumed the participation and attentiveness of the faculty beyond the confines of the classroom. Jordan strongly encouraged a pattern of congeniality and communication between the faculty and student body as a whole. In Jordan's view, "In my own education, nothing meant so much to me as the contact with a few great men whom I knew face to face."[5]

With the average age of freshmen about twenty, most of the faculty were not a great deal older than the students. The majority were under 35 and were energetic and innovative—they had to be to make up for the lack of academic facilities. With no nearby bookstores, they formed a cooperative to supply school texts from sources in San Francisco. With laboratories yet to be fully equipped, they took their students out into the field. And with an initially very modest university library of some 3,000 volumes, many made available their own personal libraries.

The pioneering faculty expected to meet spartan conditions, but they found themselves in an ironic situation: they were conscious of being "stared at" by critics expecting to see expensive professors teaching in marble halls. In reality, Jordan and the faculty continually fought with the senator, who was reluctant to give ammunition to the critics, for each minor expenditure for equipment or for books. Yet spartan conditions, housing problems, and homesickness aside, they were "under the spell of Dr. Jordan's inspiring, irresistible leadership; and no obstacle expected or unexpected could daunt the President."[6]

This primitive condition would change rapidly over the next fifteen years as the university library and campus laboratories took shape. With the creation of the departments of zoology and physiology, the fac-

ulty pressed for a biological laboratory in the Monterey Bay area. Through the efforts of Stanford trustee Timothy Hopkins, the Hopkins Seaside Laboratory opened to students, both men and women, in the summer of 1892 to supplement regular coursework in biology and to support advanced study of marine animal and plant life. The Geology Department's surveys and field trips, begun during that first summer of 1892, became a regular and popular part of the curriculum by 1902. By 1903, the new chemistry building was applauded as one of the best designed and equipped chemistry laboratories in the country.

Students were attracted to the new university for a variety of reasons, not the least of which was its location in California, the climate, the sense of adventure. But the slant toward the practical and the flexibility of the curriculum also loomed large. The majority of male students selected science, engineering, and pre-professional majors such as law. A remarkable 25 percent of the female students, compared to only 4 percent nationally, also enrolled as science majors. And of those students selecting the liberal arts, most also took coursework to qualify for a California teacher's certificate.

While he encouraged students always to consider career goals, Leland Stanford also believed there was no such thing as superfluous education. The only subject required for graduation was English. As "electives"—courses not required by one's department—all classes were open to any student intellectually ready for the work. Stanford students were offered a wide range of courses from which to choose, and many took good advantage. It was not uncommon for a student—male or female—to have a course list of English literature, biology, Greek, and Chinese history, capped with Jordan's course on evolution.

On opening day, 130 women registered at Stanford to take advantage of its commitment "to afford equal facilities and give equal advantages in the University to both sexes." Women were entering colleges in record numbers during the 1890's, representing 36 percent of the American undergraduate population. In the two decades before Stanford opened, female enrollments grew at midwestern and western public universities, bolstering the ranks of these insecure new universities and bringing in desperately needed additional tuition revenues. But women usually were admitted into departments or schools separately from men and often did not qualify for the same curriculum and graduation privileges.

The surge of the 1890's particularly distressed those doubtful of women's physical strength and intellectual capacity not only to make it through college but to benefit from the opportunity. Stanford's fully coeducational setting, where the men and women shared classrooms and followed the same coursework and requirements, was heavily criticized by those who saw a distinctive difference between men's and women's educational needs. President Jordan strongly argued, however, that the coeducational system did not dilute the quality of men's education. Rather, the men

learned to be more responsible members of society due to the company of women, while women students were encouraged to develop self-confidence and clearer life goals.

Stanford University was not suggesting, however, that female students would graduate to take on male careers in a man's world. "Success" and "direct usefulness" for women remained quite traditional. "It is true that most men in college look forward to professional training and that very few women do so," wrote Jordan. "The highest product of social evolution is the growth of a civilized home, the home that only a wise, cultivated, and high-minded woman can make. To furnish such a woman is one of the worthiest functions of higher education."[7]

The Stanford students of the 1890's were drawn from across the country, but mostly from the West and Midwest. They came from similar socioeconomic and ethnic backgrounds—predominantly the middle and lower-middle classes and mixed European backgrounds. Many worked before attending Stanford and could not afford the more expensive fees of the University of California, much less those of other private universities. Expectations of college life were vague since the majority of students were the first of their families to attend college.

What these students found at Stanford was a university both socially and physically under construction. The bare bones of an academic program were in place, but student support services and a university-administered financial aid program were inventions of the future. There was no student union or bookstore, no dean of students or housing office. Admissions, registration, curriculum, and entrance exams were handled by the president, the registrar, and the faculty.

Two dormitories were completed in the summer of 1891 to house the 200 students expected to arrive that fall. The dormitories—Encina for the men, and Roble (later renamed Sequoia Hall) for the women—were owned and operated separately by the Stanford Estate as any other Stanford property rather than by the university. Residents were provided the essential comforts of board and lodging, heat and light, for $23 a month (1892). The Stanford Estate business manager was not always sympathetic to student needs, however—as a money-saving measure, one manager turned off the electricity at 9 P.M. until students and faculty protested that they could hardly study by candlelight.

Originally, two sandstone dormitories of equal size were planned. Construction of the men's dormitory began early in 1891 as Stanford reconsidered the recommendation of one of his academic advisors, M.I.T. president Francis A. Walker, to begin the university without admitting women and without the attendant questions and publicity of coeducation. Stanford hesitated to take this advice, and his new president David Starr Jordan vocally opposed it. Jordan credited Mrs. Stanford with the final outcome. Persuaded, somewhat reluctantly, by her husband that the university should be coeducational, she backed President Jordan and insisted that it be so from the beginning. At the end of the summer, Roble Hall was quickly built of reinforced concrete rather than sandstone to make it ready for opening day.

The two dormitories could house less than half the student body. Experiencing the university's first housing shortage, the remaining students made do by boarding in the nearby farm towns of Mayfield and Menlo Park, in newly born Palo Alto, or with faculty families lucky to live on campus.

Social life was neither complicated nor enriched by racial or cultural diversity typical of American universities of the later twentieth century. While Senator Stanford encouraged the sons and daughters of Chinese ranch workers and of the Irish and black servants to attend the university, apparently only one black student registered. Foreign students, particularly from Japan, far outnumbered American-born minorities. The growing number of Japanese students—7 in 1891, 19 by 1900—resulted in a healthy Japanese Student Association, sponsored by Jordan and other faculty with strong interests in Pan-Pacific relations. Each year the rolls of registered students would include a small but growing number who listed their birthplace as Japan, Canada, Mexico, China, England, Scotland, Ireland, or France, with a few from Australia and New Zealand. No records were kept of racial background of American-born applicants.

Although campus social life was not challenged by significant socioeconomic or racial diversity, the students, especially the men, assumed that social stratification was reflected by the selection of housing. At the ostensibly democratic university, a class system grew based on where the student chose to, or could afford to, live—dormitory, fraternity, sorority, boarding house, or shacks of "the Camp." But perhaps echoing Leland Stanford's distrust of the "educational millinery" of the colleges of the rich, student society initially took on a style of its own, a "reverse class system" as a visitor from Harvard described it, passionate in its support of the common man, disdainful of the nobler aspects of culture. The cult of the "Roughs," or "Barbarians," soon challenged the elitist notions of the

"Frats." A subculture dominant in Encina Hall, the "Roughs" were the kings of roughhousing and hazing, shunning such symbols of civilization as clean corduroys. Ignoring the benefits of coeducation, they preferred a "beer bust" in Mayfield and a smoke back at Encina with the boys to a dance with a Stanford coed.

The Associated Students of Stanford University (ASSU), organized in 1891 as the representative organization of the student body, was dominated by the men of Encina Hall until challenged in mid-decade by the growing number of fraternity men. Five fraternities had established chapters on or near campus within the first year. By 1898, the number increased to seventeen. Political power became hotly contested between the "Greeks" of the growing fraternity row and the men of Encina.

Rugged individualists, men who could not afford to live at Encina or neighboring boarding houses, much less at a fraternity, could live at the Camp, the abandoned primitive lodging occupied by construction workers of the early campus. Left largely to their own devices for board and furnishings, students could live in the barracks for about $8 a month. The Stanfords consistently ignored complaints by visitors about the unsightly whitewashed buildings, recognizing a need for some sort of affordable housing for the poorer student. The Camp stood until torn down late in the 1890's to make way for construction of the Outer Quadrangle.

Many Stanford men, and some women, worked at least part-time to pay living costs, finding jobs in faculty homes and offices or locally. The average wage for manual labor was about fifteen cents an hour. The need to work was most keenly felt by the men of the Camp, who never felt entirely free of the stigma of their poverty. Yet the Camp became a symbol of the opportunity provided by the university. Men of the Camp reaped a campus success out of proportion to their numbers and self-image: six successive editorships of the student newspaper, the *Daily Palo Alto*, and, by 1899, nine of eleven campus first prizes for poetry and fiction.

Although the first sorority, Kappa Alpha Theta,

was established early in 1892, the number of sororities grew more slowly than fraternities, with only three established by 1898. In part this may have been because the pioneer women associated together more freely in spite of residence and formed sorority-like groups regardless of the location of living accommodations. Less influenced by the dormitory-Greek dichotomy and effectively excluded from the heated political contests over control of the ASSU, student publications, and key societies, Stanford women watched the political power play from a distance. Lacking larger political power, the women concentrated on their own activities and on monitoring a general sense of propriety and order among themselves.

The Stanford women were well aware that they were being watched by critics of coeducation for any sign of unladylike behavior or any infringement on male expectations of college life. Working within those bounds, the women were determined to take full advantage of academic, social, and athletic opportunities. Well organized and involved in extracurricular activities, the women quickly gained an impressive reputation for scholastic accomplishment and for social and financial responsibility.

In its first academic year of 1891–92, the Stanford student body included a full set of classes from freshman to senior and a small number of graduate students. The older students as well as the faculty brought with them experiences and expectations of college life and spurred the creation of organizations similar to those they had known elsewhere. By the fall of 1892, two literary societies promoted literary training but limited their membership; the Biology, Zoology, and Geology clubs featured research papers of faculty and students; each class was organized politically, and students participated in lively debates through the Republican Club and Democratic Club. A Glee Club (men's) was led by Professor Morris of San Francisco, and a band of eighteen members contemplated becoming a military band.

By the end of the decade, clubs had blossomed. Students supported six literary societies (five exclusively male), a press club, several law societies, a symphony, a glee club, two mandolin clubs (male and female), and a band. Civil and electrical engineering both joined the list of science clubs.

Other organizations sprang up to fill various needs. Since the university provided no health services, the volunteer Student Guild, organized in 1895, built an infirmary and promoted the general health of the students. The Young Men's and Women's Christian Associations opened chapters within the first year. In addition to encouraging religious observance and proper conduct, the YMCA annually published the university's only student handbook, for decades Stanford's best compilation of information on the academic program, student organizations, and university facilities.

Without the distractions of an urban campus and with mobility limited by the expense of traveling to San Francisco or San Jose, entertainment and other cultural activities were predominantly local and centered on living groups and clubs. Outside groups, however, were warmly welcomed and sought after by the student clubs, and political debates, lectures, and recitals by visitors willing to come to the Farm were well attended.

Receptions and dances hosted by the dormitories, fraternities, and sororities and get-togethers with faculty provided a special glue for the new community of strangers gathered from across the West and Midwest. They also served as opportunities for faculty and administrators to encourage and teach proper behavior. Propriety was as much self-enforced by the students as it was promoted by the faculty. The customs of the larger world of middle America—the proper introductions, orderly dance cards, and modes of appropriate behavior in mixed company—were conscientiously observed by all but the unrepentant "Roughs" of Encina Hall, under the watchful eye of the faculty and especially faculty wives.

The presence of Leland and Jane Stanford was strongly felt by the students and faculty as the Stanfords interspersed Washington, D.C., political and social duties with attendance at university functions. Students and faculty were often welcomed with informal receptions at the Stanford residence on campus. Senator and Mrs. Stanford took an active, if somewhat confused and amused, interest in the welfare and activities of "their" students, and the students were equally bemused and impressed with the older couple. Following Senator Stanford's death in 1893, Mrs. Stanford especially appreciated the attention of the students, hosting groups of students at the Palo Alto residence or groups of alumni when she traveled.

Aside from creative yet respectful interpretations of Stanford family activities, the campus had to create its own myths and legends. The students reveled in the growing public fascination with the romanticism of Spanish California. They enjoyed the tales of local personalities, particularly Peter Coutts, the "mysterious Frenchman," credited with a past of European intrigue, a cache of riches, and odd ideas about farming. Jordan enjoyed the Coutts legend as much as the students, and during Jordan "at-homes" he dramatized and embellished the inaccurate Coutts legends for the

entertainment of the students. Coutts was, in fact, the well-educated banker Jean-Baptiste Paulin Caperon. The urbane Frenchman had come to Mayfield in 1873, introduced Ayrshire and Holstein-Friesian dairy cattle to the country, and developed one of the most productive dairies in the state. In 1882, Coutts returned to France, and Stanford purchased his "Ayrshire Farm," which adjoined Stanford's property, operating it as the "Running Ranch." The Coutts home, named Escondite Cottage by Jordan, became the university's first presidential residence.

Music and drama loomed large in Stanford community life even though there were no academic departments teaching the subjects, no theater or auditorium, no one in the student body or faculty with formal theatrical training. Just as Stanford's first varsity football players quickly learned a game that only half of them had ever seen played, so did the actors and actresses, musicians, directors, and stage managers learn the crafts of dramatics and musical performance in action.

The first theatrical performance was a farce introducing the light verse of Charles K. Field, '95, held without scenery in the small chapel of the Inner Quad. This primitive setting was immediately set aside when someone discovered the possibilities of the men's gymnasium. For ten years the center of student dramatic productions, the gym could be transformed after its last afternoon class into a theater—a knockdown stage replaced the floor apparatus; a drop curtain was pulled out from its storage in the loft; scenery went into temporary frames; electricians rigged up lights, and windows were covered; portable bleachers were brought in from the baseball field and spare chairs from the Quad. All was disassembled before classes began the next morning.

With productions long on energy but short on funds, most profits went to staging or costumes. Sets were repainted, reversed, cut down, and built back up through the years to save money for costumes of an Elizabethan play or a deck for the H.M.S. Pinafore.

Nearly everything in the dramatic line was tried, from farce to Greek tragedy. Commended for their nerve as much as for the quality of their performance, the English Club won Bay Area critical acclaim for its 1903 production of the Elizabethan play The Knight of the Burning Pestle, as "daringly successful" as the previous year's production of Antigone by the Department of Greek.

More reflective of college life of the times were the many original plays, farces, and musicals written and produced by Stanford students. Dormitory groups, fraternities, and clubs competed for space in the gymnasium and, after 1899, in the new, fully equipped Assembly Hall in the Outer Quadrangle. The class plays were riddled with comic interpretations of students and faculty of the day and elaborately staged inside jokes, a tradition maintained in today's Big Game Gaieties of Ram's Head.

Music also had its serious and light sides. The Symphony Orchestra and the Band, the Girls' Mandolin Club, and the Girls' Glee Club entertained on campus, while the all-male Stanford Glee Club and the Mandolin Club toured the Pacific Coast from San Francisco to Vancouver throughout the decade. On the other hand, there was the Milpitas Brass Bugle Club, a creative group of students who combined harp, lute, and flute with bass drum, harmonica, and "Jew's harp." Their motto: "It is better to have arrived from Milpitas than to have never arrived at all."

Enterprising student editors lost little time getting into print. Stanford's first campus publication, the monthly Palo Alto, was sold to attendees at opening day, October 1, 1891. Aiming at a wider readership, editor Holbrook Blinn unsuccessfully suggested a coalition with editors at the University of California. Never truly representative of the Stanford campus, the monthly folded in less than a year, giving way to its competition—the Sequoia.

The Sequoia was established in 1891 as a biweekly news and literary journal published by the ASSU. During its first year, it was much like an official organ of any small private college, reporting on mundane activities of the students, such as how "the young ladies attending church at Mayfield Sunday evenings are becoming fence climbers," or "Cole says that engineers are a tough sort of crowd anyway." Though the first issues depended greatly on faculty for weightier contributions, the Sequoia soon included student essays, fiction, and poetry of increasing quality. By its second year it turned decisively towards literature, leaving the news function to the newly born Daily Palo Alto.

The Daily Palo Alto, or "Dippy," had no literary pretensions—it filled the niche for news and filled it well. Highly successful from its first issue in September 1892, the newspaper was well run and won a reputation for temperate and accurate reporting. Many of its editors and reporters moved on to larger newspapers in San Francisco and other American cities. The Daily Palo Alto changed its name to the Stanford Daily in 1926 and has remained in continuous operation for almost 100 years.

The fall of 1899 saw the introduction of the Chaparral. A journal of wit and humor at best and colorful bad taste in lesser moments, the "Chappie" replaced Josh, a Stanford-U.C. publication that represented the humorous side of campus life on both sides of the Bay but that had folded in 1897. The Chaparral evolved from a discussion during a boring psychology lecture between Bristow Adams, then publisher of the Sequoia and later a Cornell professor, and Everett Smith, who would later be a professor of journalism at Stanford. From a precarious beginning, it soon became one of early Stanford's most popular publications.

The campus yearbook, the Stanford Quad, was created by the Pioneer Class of '95 during its junior year, and the Quad would continue to be published by the junior class until 1927. Its name was chosen because of "its snap and vigour—a marked characteristic of the University" and because it embodied the nucleus of the university settlement and sentiment—the Quadrangle.

Searching for its particular niche, each *Quad* of the pioneer years tried a different specialty—literary contests, humorous ribbing, artistic contributions. By the tenth volume in 1903, with the *Sequoia* and the *Chaparral* settled in, the editors sensed an end of an era of experimentation. Volume 10 was a careful record of student activities from the beginning, setting a tone of conservative summation and reporting that would be followed for decades.

Stanford's setting amid foothills in a temperate climate was a year-round invitation to outdoor activity. The foothills and nearby mountains attracted hikers, bicyclists, and casual strollers. But as popular as such outdoor exercise was among students and faculty, these activities could not take the place of competitive sports in college life.

Athletics in American colleges and universities first had been organized in the 1870's, centering on baseball, football, and rowing. Teams and rules were constructed, but the players were strictly amateur, recruited from the ranks of the student body and destined for careers in business or the professions, not sports. Baseball was Stanford's first sport, a game that could be quickly set up on the dirt field behind Encina with equipment brought from home. The young faculty could not resist getting involved. A match game between the seniors and faculty, with President Jordan

at first base, was played in November 1891, drawing the university community's attention to the need for some sort of athletic field.

Though at first facilities were limited, plans for future playing fields and gymnasiums were ambitious—and perpetually underfunded. The university administration was heartily in favor of sports but saw its primary role as the promotion of its students' health and strength. Competitive athletics were left in the hands of the Associated Students. Two "temporary" frame gymnasiums were built by 1892; enrollment in gymnasium classes was large, partly because of an innovative university policy—credit was given for gym classes as for any other class. Additional activities were sponsored by various men's and women's clubs.

In the 1890's, football replaced baseball nationally as the leading intercollegiate spectator sport, where college heroes were made and "college spirit" whipped up student emotions and alumni loyalty. Stanford had no equipment, no coach, and no team until a group of undergraduates got together to play on the stubble field behind Encina. Few of the players had ever seen the game played until they were joined by the several upperclassmen transfers who had played on college teams the year before. A clash with the University of California was inevitable, and a challenge from across the Bay was heartily accepted. Since Stanford was unable to field a team during the fall semester, a date in March 1892 was set.

As a new institution with a new student body and no athletic program, Stanford faced Cal's established tradition and considerable athletic record. No one expected Stanford to seek intercollegiate competition within its first year, but popular interest in Stanford's future was high and comparison to the state university common. Thus this first contest came to represent much more than an afternoon's entertainment. The Stanford team hoped at least to hold its own by making a respectable showing, proving that Stanford could field a competitive team; the Berkeley team, tired of the popular attention paid to the upstart university across the Bay, hoped to take its presumptuous opponent down a peg.

As with many future "Big Games," the contest was exciting and the outcome unpredictable as the underdog battled the overconfident favorite. Much to everyone's surprise, Stanford won 14 to 10. More than a single victory, the game set the tone of intercollegiate competition between the two universities as Cal and Stanford determined to meet year after year on equal footing in athletics and academics alike.

One of Stanford's longest-held traditions, its cardinal red color, came to life during the first Big Game. As early as October 1891, students vocalized a need for college colors around which they could rally. Many American colleges—at least those fielding popular football teams—were selecting official colors of combat to distinguish sides and instill pride. The editor of the monthly *Palo Alto* urged gold—the premier metal and closely tied to California—and white; the weekly *Sequoia* supported the idea of cardinal red, "the color of conquest." The student body was roughly divided, and the battle was fought out by the two student newspapers. In the end, white and gold fell by the wayside as too much like the blue and gold of California. Vibrant cardinal banners, flowers, and ribbons bedecked San Francisco in marked contrast to Berkeley's blue and gold. Headlines in newspapers up and down the West Coast shouted that the Blue and Gold

had bowed to the Cardinal. The decision, helped along by the news media, was made.

Other sports—track and field, basketball, soccer, swimming, fencing—came along as facilities and fields improved, but these were aimed primarily at the needs and interests of the male students. Stanford coeds were expected to be spectators, rarely participants, of combative college sport. A gymnasium was considered adequate for the women, with an emphasis on exercise and good health, not competition. While the head of the Physical Education Department encouraged women to take up outdoor exercise, it was the Women's Athletic Club (later the Women's Athletic Association) that promoted competitive sport.

Basketball was the game ultimately chosen for women's competition, with the first game held in 1894 with Castilleja School in Palo Alto. Stanford lost 13 to 14. Two years later, a challenge was sent to the women of the University of California. This game was held in San Francisco, April 4, 1896, with only women permitted as spectators as it was considered improper for men to watch the women cavorting in their gym suits. Playing before the days of backboards and one-handed shooting, Stanford won by the score of 2 to 1.

The fertile imagination and sense of humor of Stanford undergraduates provided a continual source of entertainment affectionately termed "college spirit," such as the circus-like initiations into farcical societies, fake examinations imposed on freshmen, and nightshirt parades past the windows of Roble Hall. But none of these pranks captured the imagination quite like the rituals grounded in rivalry—from the rivalries between juniors and seniors, and between the "Pioneer Class" of '95 and the class of '96, to the ever-present competition with the University of California.

Although class hats—the senior field hat or "sombrero," the junior smashed top hat or "plug," the sophomore red felt "dink," the freshman beanie— were not a Stanford invention but already prevalent at

its sister university across the Bay, the "Plug Ugly" confrontation was intrinsically Stanford. The Plug Ugly, a hat-smashing melee between the seniors and juniors for control of the Inner Quadrangle, followed immediately after the Plug Ugly play, a highly satirical burlesque that took literal and provoking potshots at the seniors, individually and collectively. So entertained were the audience and participants at the first presentation in 1898 that future junior classes turned it into a yearly ritual. The shows soon aimed wider, offending faculty and administration as well as seniors, and heads as well as hats were smashed. The juniors' plugs, painted with layers of heavy lead paint beneath the elaborate decoration, came in handy as clubs, and the Plug Ugly itself became a glorified brawl. The traditional junior-senior clash would last fifteen years before being abolished in 1913.

The Stanford Axe is perhaps the most graphic symbol of the Stanford-Berkeley competition. It gained attention when taken by Cal after a series of indignities suffered by Stanford in 1899. The school year began with the first loss to Cal in the annual varsity football game, and Stanford teams continued to lose in other competitions as the year progressed. April capped the losing streak. First, Stanford's highly acclaimed debating team lost to the UC team in a close judgment. Then, adding insult to injury, Berkeley men ran off with the Stanford Axe.

The Axe itself had innocent beginnings. In 1896, student Will Irwin produced the "Give 'em the axe" cheer that became the calling card of Stanford rooting sections. To make the cheer more realistic, an axe was flourished before the Berkeley crowd at the Stanford-Cal baseball game of April 1899 in San Francisco. The Berkeley students were not especially intimidated, nor did the Stanford crowd attach much importance to the axe until Berkeley won the game and then snatched the axe in a running battle that progressed from the playing field through the streets of San Francisco to the Berkeley ferry. Suddenly this axe, though much like any other, became a symbol, and desperate attempts immediately were made to steal it back. The axe was well hidden and remained carefully guarded until Stanford students succeeded in stealing it back 31 years later.

Frustrated in their initial attempt to regain the axe, the Stanford rescue party retaliated later that year. They targeted Cal's "senior fence." The Stanford party counterattacked by ripping out the fence under cover of night and throwing it into a wagon. Breathless with excitement and expecting a fight with furious Berkeley students at any point along the long route home, the Stanford contingent made it to the Peninsula without opposition and paraded the fence along El Camino Real and up Palm Drive to the Oval. After an exciting rally in the Quad, the fence was broken up, and rumor had it that pieces of the fence were the foundation of a glorious Big Game bonfire the next year. It turned out, however, that the fence was not much missed at Berkeley and had never been truly accepted by the majority of the seniors. A gleeful telegram arrived from two Berkeley faculty members: "Students seem thankful for removal of rubbish. [You] might sell lumber to pay expenses."

The pioneer years were epitomized as much by financial problems as by light-hearted adventures. Plagued by financial insecurity during the first half of the decade as well as by vocal critics and a skeptical public, the community was held together by the common bond of struggle and adversity.

Senator Stanford's death in 1893, shortly after the university's opening, brought to light a major deficiency in its founding—the university's income was not distinct from that of other Stanford properties. When Jordan needed money for salaries or supplies, the Senator wrote a check. With the Stanford estate tied up in probate proceedings, the checks stopped.

Jane Stanford, as administrator of the Stanford estate, found herself faced with uncooperative business partners (particularly railroad president Collis P. Huntington) and legatees demanding their allotted share from the will as well as a severe business depression affecting all of the Stanford estate's major investments. To make matters worse, the federal government filed suit against the estate for Leland Stanford's presumed share of construction loans originally made to the Central Pacific Railroad. Although the loans were not yet due, the government acted on rumors that Huntington intended to default.

Against the advice of her business managers, the shy 65-year-old Jane Stanford refused to close the university. During the probate proceedings (which lasted more than five years) she was allowed to spend from the estate her normal household allotment—$10,000 a month to run three large residences with seventeen servants. She convinced the probate judge that the

faculty were, in fact, her "servants." She reduced her own staff from seventeen to three, reduced her spending to only $350 a month, and gave the remaining $9,650 to Jordan for monthly faculty salaries. She did not limit herself to this domestic stopgap; she took a hard look at the "experimental" farm properties and put the Vina Ranch on a profit-making basis for the first time.

By 1896, the federal court suit was won by the Stanford estate. The financial security of the university was again assured as the probate proceedings were completed. A gleeful crowd of students, faculty, and staff gathered in the Inner Quadrangle to hear the announcement of the court decision, and Jordan told the students that in celebration they could do anything but paint the professors or tear down buildings. Late that evening, a group of students painted the campus Post Office cardinal red.

The relationship that developed between Mrs. Stanford and President Jordan throughout the 1890's was not always a smooth one: she was intensely practical, he a perennial optimist; she thought in terms of buildings and financial support, he in terms of academic program.

As the century turned, bedrock Stanford family practicality had the edge. Mrs. Stanford—now the check writer—favored holding the line on expansion of academic programs and the size of the student body in order to complete the physical plant. Jordan acquiesced, and so began the era he called "Stanford's Stone Age." The building of the memorial campus would take on renewed energy.

Mrs. Stanford's authority was most visibly evidenced in her modification of the look of the campus. A remarkable style had been set with the quadrangle plan of Frederick Law Olmsted and the elegant Romanesque sandstone arcades of Charles Coolidge, but Mrs. Stanford preferred large, neoclassical buildings individually sited along the flanks of the Oval. Construction of two large buildings—a gymnasium and a new library—would begin east of the Oval after the turn of the century to counterbalance the museum and the chemistry building to the west.

In 1899, Mrs. Stanford also made the first radical change in the university's academic policy by limiting the number of women who could enroll at one time to 500. At Stanford, closely associated in the mind of the public with the success story of coeducation, the percentage of women in the student body had risen from 25 percent to almost 45 percent within its first eight years. Stanford was not alone in experiencing this increase—by the end of the century, more women were graduating from high school than men, and many looked to the coeducational colleges of the West. At the University of California the percentage similarly had risen from 27 percent in 1891 to 44 percent by 1899. But critics of coeducation grew more vocal during the late 1890's as the number of women in higher education dramatically increased. They assumed that money spent on courses attractive to women, usually the humanities, was taken from money that could more properly be spent on professional education—engineering, law, medicine. Although proud of the accomplishments of her women students, Mrs. Stanford felt strongly that the educational needs of the men must predominate, and she feared that men would be discouraged from attending Stanford if its program devoted significant resources to the women.

Mrs. Stanford's right to set the limitation was unquestioned, but the optimistic Jordan and registrar Elliott continued to press for a higher limit or a percentage. Mrs. Stanford stubbornly answered, "I want the percentage of male students to greatly increase during the next five or six years. The University must be a place for men."[8]

Modifications in academic policy, the growth and change of the student body, changes in the look of the campus—all were part of the maturation of the campus community. The sense of newness and adventure had passed. A growing number of alumni looked back fondly at the years of struggle and experimentation that forged the community.

Yet the new century also brought great promise and a sense of security and success. The university had grown quickly and had established a reputation in the biological sciences, geology, and engineering. In 1891, many of its 23 original departments had been staffed by only one professor or lecturer. By the turn of the century, the faculty had filled out, and—particularly through the work of Jordan, an eminent ichthyologist, and his colleagues in the biological sciences, geologist John Casper Branner, and Charles and Guido Marx in engineering—it had shown that it could compete with the more mature academic programs of the University of California and Cornell. Its commitment to a professional curriculum was well established in its engineering, geology (mining), law, and education departments while its elective system provided a full range of selection in the sciences, humanities, and social sciences for the experimenting undergraduate.

Just over a decade after its opening, with the memorial campus virtually complete, the university celebrated the 1903 opening of the Memorial Church with pomp and ceremony. The church in itself symbolized the university's world view of openness and individuality. Although the building, with its ornate Venetian mosaics and stained glass windows, was situated at the heart of the university in the focal point of the Quadrangle, church attendance was strictly voluntary. Much to the confusion of the public, especially local ministers, its services were to be nondenominational, and representatives of local Protestant, Catholic, and Jewish congregations were variously called to speak from the pulpit. Chaplain D. Charles Gardner explained, "our anxiety is to make its services varied, simple, and spiritual in character and meaning. Being an undenominational church, it must avoid the things which divide, and exalt the principles upon which we can all agree. Thus we say no creed. We know nothing of the ceremonial. . . . Many students do not care for church services. But the church cares for them."[9]

A visitor views the young university from Palm Drive's first set of entrance gates.

Jane Stanford holds a parasol against the bright sun for her husband, Leland, as he delivers his opening day address, October 1, 1891, on the Inner Quad.

David Starr Jordan (front row, center) drew much of his youthful first faculty—including two women—from Cornell and Indiana.

Orrin Leslie Elliott, Jordan's "quiet, cautious, and courageous" first registrar and de facto dean of admissions.

"It appeared to me exactly like a factory," Ellen Coit Elliott, wife of the registrar, wrote in her memoirs.

The Stanford faculty's senior statesman, geologist John Casper Branner, was Jordan's Cornell roommate.

"The inner quadrangle was . . . like a gem in a coarse setting. How much that Inner Quad has meant to us," recalled Susan Branner, wife of the geologist.

Encina was advertised as the best equipped dormitory in the country, with hot and cold running water and dining room amenities, all for $4.50 a week.

Encina men of the Pioneer Class of '95 pose on their front doorstep for San Jose photographer Andrew P. Hill late in 1891.

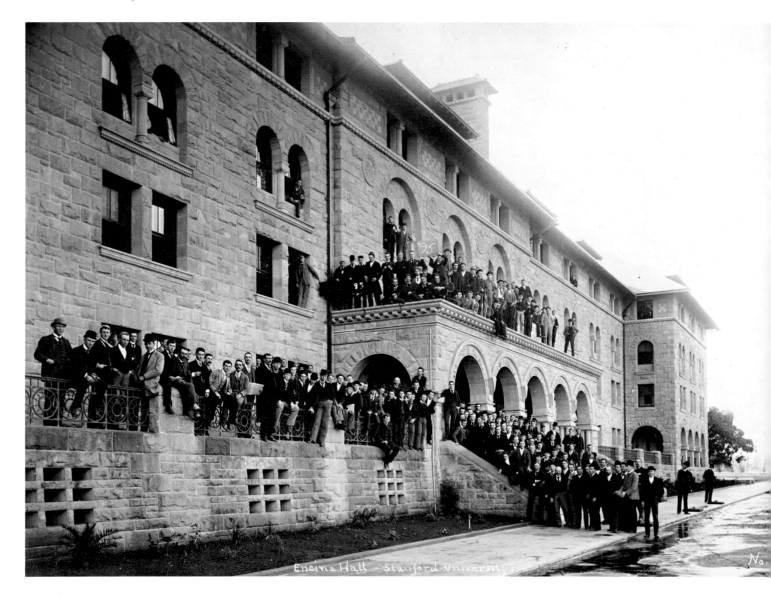

Student lodgings (right) on Alvarado Row and in Encina Hall, c. 1892 (bottom).

The oak tree adopted as its own by the Pioneer Class would come down at the end of the century to make way for Outer Quad construction.

The first Roble Hall, hastily completed before opening day, filled with young women before the construction debris could be cleaned up.

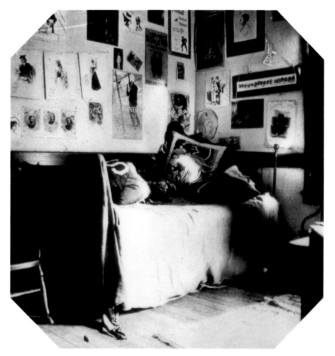

"It is good to live and learn": life in rooms 39 (left) and 19 (right) of Roble Hall as depicted in student albums of Louise Culver, '96, and Jessica Wilson, '02.

Turkey dinner at Sigma Alpha Epsilon.

Not all sororities had chapter houses or were Greek letter chapters: women of "the Combine," a socially prestigious group of Roble women, came largely from Central Valley towns.

Sigma Nu's clapboard chapter house on Alvarado was typical of fraternity houses built on campus during the 1890's.

Stanford's first sorority, Kappa Alpha Theta, rented a large older house in Mayfield for several years before moving to Alvarado Row.

The barracks of the Camp, once used as a bunkhouse for construction workers, housed a self-supporting elite of campus editors, writers, and poets.

Lauro House, offering rooms for unmarried professors, was operated by Phi Delta Theta until the fraternity could build its own chapter house. The boarding house was later renamed Madrono.

The quality of food at the dorms soon drove some students to other "digs." These four women kept house in Palo Alto and were "off to the Quad" in the spring of 1899.

Faculty children enjoy a birthday party on the porch of the Stanford Inn. The restaurant, built in 1897 on the site of today's Art Gallery, was the only public place visitors could get a bite to eat on campus at the turn of the century.

The bicycle shop, behind the engineering lab buildings, also served as telegraph office and as agency headquarters for several San Francisco newspapers.

The former Coutts library (right) had several uses— including twice as an elementary school. Miss Boring poses with her charges, sons and daughters of the pioneer faculty.

"Miss Jessie," Jessie Knight Jordan, the university's first lady, in 1900.

Peter Coutts's Escondité Cottage was home to the Jordan family until 1894. The first three applicants to take entrance exams did so on the veranda; the young woman passed, but the two men failed.

Nicknamed "the Decalogue" by students and "the Cornell Colony" by faculty, the ten pattern-book houses erected along Alvarado Row initially were unsoftened by lawn, vine, or tree. "It only needed the line of clothes flapping in the wind to complete the picture of a poor quarter in the outskirts of some western town," observed Susan Branner.

The turreted home of Professor James O. Griffin survives today on the corner of Alvarado Row and Campus Drive.

A sweeping view of campus, from the Quad south down the road to Mayfield, from treeless San Juan Hill. The community along Alvarado, Salvatierra, and Lasuen was thriving by 1900.

Mechanical engineering professor Albert W. Smith, author of "Hail, Stanford, Hail," made his home in the newborn town of Palo Alto.

Despite Mrs. Stanford's motherly worries, most students enjoyed their coeducational setting—on a walk through the arboretum, perched in an oak in the foothills, in the shade of a La Honda forest.

Students coined their own word for dating: "queening."

Faculty and students—not far separated in age—knew an easy camaraderie: Professor and Mrs. Charles H. Gilbert and student members of the Zoology Club on a picnic outing in 1898.

L.R. Weinman   E.C. Dudley   M.N. Stearns   J.F.C   Edith, Mirrielees

Stanford's first debate team won a unanimous decision against a surprised University of California team in 1893.

Sophomore Edith Mirrie-lees, '07 and future professor of English, joined the junior class staff of the 1906 "Quad" as an associate editor.

Getting away from it all, men of the Botanical Club (left) go camping in the nearby hills.

The "Sequoia" quickly gave up competing with the student newspaper, the "Daily Palo Alto," in news and sports to concentrate on things literary.

Hill & Yard

79 & 81 W. Santa Clara St.
San Jose, Cal.

The Encina Wheelmen ped-
aled their high wheelers
over rugged dirt roads to
Santa Cruz and La Honda.

"Pzhah!" The Little Ger-
man Band borrowed the
bass drum of its more con-
ventional cousin, the Stanford University Concert
Band, to play in the student
circus.

Stanford's band, here in
1895, originated in 1893,
springing from the popularity of mandolin and glee
clubs.

"Antigone," performed by students and faculty in the original Greek, received rave reviews in 1902 as much for its audacity as the fine quality of the production.

The popular Elizabethan comedy "Knight of the Burning Pestle," staged in 1903, was as much a pleasant surprise and critical hit as "Antigone" the year before.

"Trinummus, Act IV of Plautus," advertised as the first classical play staged west of the Rockies, premiered in Latin in the temporary chapel in the Inner Quad, 1892.

JUNIOR QUAD APPEARS.

Activity came to a halt on the morning the "Quad" was distributed. The campus yearbook, started by the Pioneer Class in their junior year, remained a junior class publication until 1927.

Students concentrate in drawing class and biology lab.

A summer of intensive study at Hopkins Seaside Laboratory, seen here in 1894, promoted a special sense of camaraderie among students and faculty.

Carpenter shop in the engineering lab building along Panama Street.

The first campus library, located on the Inner Quad.

Geologist James Perrin Smith (center, seated) took graduate students and a guide on an 1895 expedition into the California wilderness. Among the earliest of the summer field courses, the expedition soon became a popular tradition.

*Early faculty members, formal and informal. Opposite: (top
left) Ellwood P. Cubberley, education; (top right) Clara S.
Stoltenberg, anatomy; (center) Oliver P. Jenkins, physiology. Above, Douglas H. Campbell, botany; right, Vernon
Kellogg, entomology.*

*"Dr. Sewall, caught flirting with one of his charges (for-
merly a U.C. coed)" would one day become clinical professor
Edward Sewall, '98, M.D. Cooper Medical College '02.*

"Excellent facilities for athletics have been provided at considerable expense by the founders of the university," according to the "Leland Stanford Junior University Register," 1892. The first Roble Gym for women (above) was located some distance behind Roble Hall; the first Encina Gym for men (below), located behind Encina Hall, also hosted dramatics, concerts, dances, and assemblies.

Baseball was Stanford's first glory sport, with season after season of winning or undefeated varsity teams. Seniors square off with faculty on the stubble field behind Encina Hall, with President Jordan an acknowledged power hitter.

The popular varsity team of 1898 had a winning season.

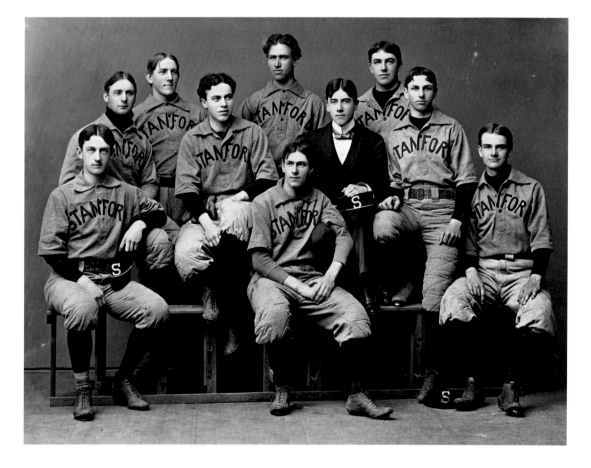

Though track and field events were slow to gain the prestige of 1890's football and baseball, their action and heroic finishes gave them dramatic advantage in photography. Below, the 1893 relay team.

Basketball captain Frances
Tucker, 1897, is inter-
viewed by a student re-
porter while captain Stella
McCray poses with her
1896 team—just returned
from winning the first
American intercollegiate
women's basketball game 2
to 1 against the University
of California.

Anne Martin, '96, intercollegiate women's singles tennis champion in 1895, later
a noted feminist speaker
and women's suffrage
activist.

Student body treasurer Herbert Hoover, '95, seen in suit and tie with the varsity football team of 1894, brought reform and unaccustomed financial responsibility to the student-operated athletics program.

The jumble of uniforms of the senior interclass football team of '95 typified the happy-go-lucky style of most Stanford athletics in the first years.

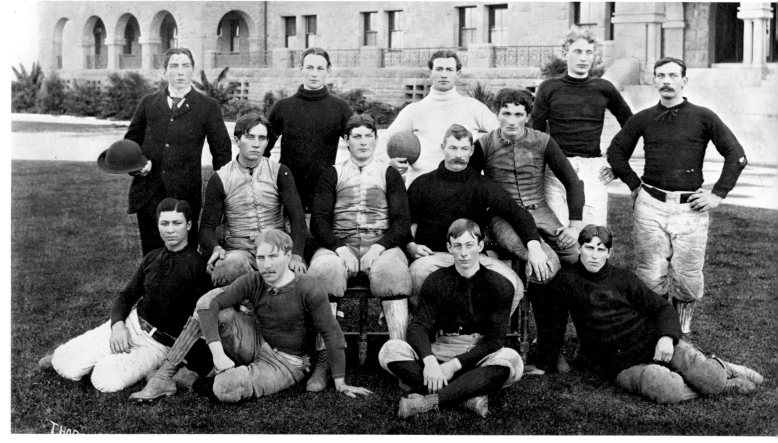

Star players Tom Williams, '97 (top), and Guy Cochran, '96 (bottom). When Cochran complained of needing new shoes, thrifty financial manager Hoover gave him new shoelaces.

James F. Lanagan, A. B. '00 in Latin, elegant in his senior sombrero in 1900. As Stanford's football coach from 1903 to 1909 he insisted on ideals of sportsmanship in an increasingly violent game.

81

Bonfires celebrated Stanford baseball as early as 1893, but in time they accompanied the frenzy before the fall Big Game and became serious business.

Stanford's informal March 1892 grudge match with the University of California—now considered the first Big Game—was played on neutral ground at the Haight Street Field in San Francisco. Cal, favored by 25 to 1, lost 14 to 10 to "Jordan's Kidlets."

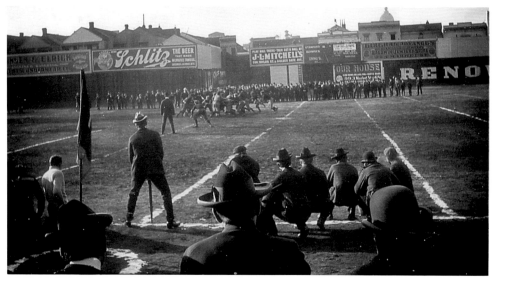

Students arrive in the Inner Quad with the Big C senior fence, stolen from the Berkeley campus in 1899 after Cal students stole Stanford's Axe earlier that year. No one in Berkeley seemed to care, and the fence disappeared into a bonfire.

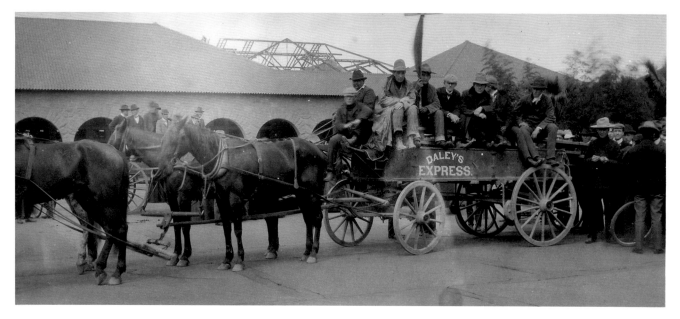

Stanford's Tournament of Roses matchup in Pasadena on New Year's Day in 1902 with "point-a-minute" Michigan was a disaster. Stanford lost 49 to 0, and the tournament turned to chariot racing until the Rose Bowl was born in 1916.

Women of '98 pose with junior class plugs. Lou Henry, later to marry geology classmate Herbert Hoover, '95, is second from left.

Cast of the Plug Ugly play of 1901. In this ancestor to the Ram's Head's Big Game Gaieties, juniors satirized with abandon university faculty and senior class student leaders.

Any excuse for a parade, or "peerade," a tradition since 1892, when Encina men marched in their nightshirts to celebrate a baseball victory.

Outings in the hills and along Steven's Creek were popular with students and faculty alike.

The one-dollar Brownie camera, widely used after its introduction in 1900, produced the round image seen in many albums.

In any state of dress, a Stanford man was rarely bareheaded.

At Roble "hen parties," or just for the fun of it, Stanford women delighted in clowning—and ribbing the Stanford roughs.

Gov. STANFORD.

The importance of academic degrees was spoofed at commencement by Richard K. Culver, '99, brother of the future dean of men George Culver, '97.

Many a Stanford rough worked for a living before and while attending Stanford—for decades, their informality set the style.

A favorite setting for a snapshot: Roble Bridge over San Francisquito Creek, where legend had it more marriage proposals were made than anywhere else on campus.

When called upon, Stanford men could look surprisingly dapper on the Inner Quad.

Applauded by Jordan for their civilizing influence, Stanford women took just as readily to the code of camaraderie and informality.

A group of Roble women pose in their finery at the Inner Quad site reserved for Memorial Church, 1894.

The death of Senator Stanford shortly after commencement in June 1893 left the university financially troubled and on uncertain legal grounds.

Stanford's funeral cortege winds its way from the Inner Quadrangle to the new Stanford Mausoleum in the arboretum, near the "Arizona" cactus garden. Floral contributions included a locomotive from the Brotherhood of Locomotive Engineers.

Jane Stanford, now sole administrator of the Stanford estate, waged a five-year battle for the financial security of the university against a business depression, a lawsuit by the federal government, and uncooperative railroad partners.

With the return of financial security in 1898, President Jordan hoped to expand the academic program. However Mrs. Stanford, at the helm, was determined to complete the physical plant of the memorial campus.

The towering Memorial Arch, main entry to the Quad, was erected in 1900. Stone-carvers took almost three more years to add its ambitious frieze depicting "The Progress of Civilization in America."

Memorial Church was completed in 1903. An unlabeled photo from the album of resident architect Charles Hodges shows what may be the 1903 visit of representatives of the Venetian firm of Salviatti and Co. Mrs. Stanford walked the scaffolds during construction, testing with the end of her parasol to make sure the carvings were deep enough.

Mrs. Stanford deviated from the quadrangle plan to build large neoclassical buildings along the flanks of the Oval such as the new men's gymnasium, below, which stood directly across from the museum. From the gym roof can be seen, from left to right, Roble Hall, the chemistry building, and the museum.

The rotunda dome of the library taking shape early in 1906.

Jane Stanford built the first phase of the museum envisioned by her son in 1891. The addition of three wings enclosing a quadrangle made it the largest privately owned museum in the country.

The memorial campus nearly complete, Mrs. Stanford devoted more of her time to world travel in order to build the museum's collections and to visit her alumni-children. She was photographed in Egypt and in 1904 posing with alumni in Japan.

From high on Alta Vista, the residence of Mrs. Stanford's brother Charles Lathrop, one could see across a placid Lagunita to the campus below.

Adolescence, 1903-1916

Let us not be afraid to outgrow old thoughts and ways, and dare to think on new lines as to the future of the work under our care. Let us not be poor copies of other universities.   JANE STANFORD
Address to the Board of Trustees, July 1904

When the freshmen of the class of '06 arrived in the fall of 1902, the future of Stanford University couldn't have looked brighter. They had no idea they would be dubbed the "Calamity Class."

No class had entered under happier conditions. The financial crisis of the 1890's was past. The largest class yet, '06 was the first to play the freshman "Big Game" on the University of California's new athletic field instead of on borrowed turf in San Francisco.

A new era of prosperity was visible in the very look of the campus as Mrs. Stanford poured her energy and resources into completing the Quadrangle and adding large, new buildings in the Quad's "front yard." New wings to the Leland Stanford Junior Museum made it the largest privately owned museum in the United States. And the towering Memorial Arch, dedicated to the progress of civilization, loomed over the entrance of the Outer Quadrangle. Much to Jane Stanford's pleasure, the focal point of the spectacular drive up the grand avenue of Palm Drive was the newly completed Memorial Church, opened in January 1903.

Alumnus Leo Stanley later wrote that as he and a friend "walked toward the Quad, I realized that neither of us had ever seen such splendor—the sandstone buldings, the Circle bordered with red geraniums, the wonderfully laid-out grounds. All we had been accustomed to in our grain-producing village in the Upper Salinas Valley were small wooden buildings, the largest of which was the livery stable."[1]

Yet the class of 1906 would see not only the culmination of the Stanford memorial campus but its seeming collapse—and they would face not one but three springs disrupted by tragedy. During their four years at Stanford, there would be only one full-dress commencement, and theirs would be the only class to leave with no parting ceremonies at all.

The typhoid epidemic of 1903 struck in April. Two students became sick, then others from their fraternity, then several students living in Palo Alto, then students from Encina. Within weeks, 200 cases of typhoid were diagnosed. Resources were limited to two overworked doctors and the Student Guild, the voluntary student health service, with no money in its treasury and little experience. There was no university hospital, and no fully equipped hospital closer than San Francisco, where the infected were unwelcome.

With no one to rely on, the community rallied quickly. Within hours of the first diagnosed cases, Frank Hess, a senior and the new president of the Student Guild, gathered members and commandeered medicines and supplies. The top floor of Encina became a ward for male students, a boarding house in Palo Alto the women's ward. Doctors Ray Lyman Wilbur, part-time university physician, and William Snow, associate professor of hygiene, both of them Stanford alumni, spent long hours treating patients at the two student wards, moving on to private homes on campus and in town, then back to the wards.

Mrs. Stanford immediately contributed $1,000 to the student effort and offered to pay for as many professional nurses as were needed. But nurses were in short supply throughout the Peninsula, and students filled their places, trained in the rudiments of nursing by the few available professionals.

Their initiative and hard work paid off. Of the 200 stricken, only eight died, a much smaller percentage than among those cared for at home. None of the volunteers became infected, due in part to the very liberal use of disinfectants. Within a month, the makeshift hospitals were empty, and classes were back to normal. However, self-supporting students who had been sick were now faced with both the loss of income and heavy expenses. The Faculty Committee on Graduation cut its program and directed the savings to the expenses of the needy students. Following the committee's example, the senior class gave up the coveted, and expensive, highlight of Senior Week—the Senior Ball and sunrise breakfast—to add to the fund so that no student would be forced to leave school because of the costs of illness.

The university learned a lesson. Bolstering the strongly held belief in Stanford self-reliance, membership in the Student Guild became compulsory, fees were increased to assure an emergency fund, and an improvised hospital was set up in Palo Alto to serve campus and town alike.

The second shadow to hang over the Calamity Class came with the death of Jane Stanford in 1905. Two years earlier, in 1903, the 75-year-old Mrs. Stanford judged her work in finishing the physical campus as a suitable memorial to her son to be completed. She transferred her powers as surviving founder to the university's Board of Trustees. Although she was promptly elected to membership and presidency of the Board, she was determined to continue her travels to Asia, the Middle East, and Europe and further to build the collections of the Leland Stanford Junior Museum.

Mrs. Stanford had always enjoyed entertaining students in the earlier years of the university, but her travels took her away from the undergraduates for increasing amounts of time. After the century turned, students on campus saw little of her as she visited the growing number of her "Stanford family" of alumni around the world, particularly in the Pacific basin and Asia.

In the winter of 1905, Mrs. Stanford, ill with a heavy cold, set sail for Honolulu, where she died on February 28. The confusion over the cause of her death—terminal pneumonia, heart attack, rumored strychnine poisoning—caused such controversy that an autopsy was performed at Cooper Medical College in San Francisco by its senior physicians. They determined the cause to be natural, a ruptured coronary artery.

Throughout California, flags hung at half staff in Mrs. Stanford's honor. Both houses of the state legislature adjourned on March 1. On campus, classes were dismissed and all social functions canceled or postponed. The *Daily Palo Alto* published an extensive memorial issue and bordered the pages of each of its issues in black until the day of her funeral in Memorial Church. Struck by the import of Mrs. Stanford's death but now distant from Leland and Jane Stanford, the undergraduates worried about the rest of the semester. Commencement would surely be curtailed, but were classes suspended for the rest of the semester or until after the funeral? Would they be able to have Senior Week and the Senior Ball that was missed two years before?

With Mrs. Stanford's funeral in early 1905, the direct link between the university and its founders was broken. Students entering the freshman class the next fall would have a distinctly different sense of university history and loyalty and, consequently, of their own identity as the next generation.

Yet for many Stanford generations, it would be the undergraduates who would carry on one of the few long-held traditions closely linked with the Stanford family. Beginning in March 1905, members of the Senior Class placed flowers weekly before the bronze doors of the Stanford family mausoleum in the university's arboretum, adding a flower wreath each Founders' Day. The tradition of weekly flowers died eventually, but the placing of the wreath at Founders' Day by the senior class continues today, interrupted only by a brief hiatus in the 1970's.

For faculty and staff members, whether they had known the Stanfords personally or not, the sense of loss was much stronger. Senator and Mrs. Stanford had wielded tremendous influence on the development of the university. They set its tone and defined its ambitions. And they lent romantic color not only to the university's founding but to its idealist goals and brashly confident self-image. Following Senator Stan-

ford's death, Mrs. Stanford provided a sense of strength and security. Ray Lyman Wilbur later wrote: "Whenever she returned home from one of her frequent trips one could feel the fresh impulse given to everything on the campus. The hammers seemed to hit the nails oftener and the lawn mowers turn faster. . . . She had a commanding presence and a friendly dignity which only a great heart, courage and strong character and convictions can give."[2]

The faculty faced a highly conservative Board of Trustees unused to independent action. For several years, Jordan had struggled with Mrs. Stanford and the Board over student discipline and organization of the faculty. And he did not look forward to continuing the battle he had waged previously with Mrs. Stanford over the balance of funds for construction with those for academic programs and faculty salaries. Faculty salaries had yet to return to the national standard, much less their originally impressive level, since the financial crisis of the 1890's, and the faculty remembered bitterly the trade of academic program for architecture. "There are two universities," Jordan wrote, "one as seen by the faculty, the other as seen by the Board. I try to ride both horses as it were. They will coalesce sooner or later, but I may fall between."[3]

However, within a year after Mrs. Stanford's death, the outlook brightened somewhat when the Board announced that the building program was to be completed by spring of 1906 and the budget for program and salaries would be increased. In March of 1906, Harvard scholar and visiting professor William James described Stanford's bright future in his Founders' Day address. Sensing the unease of the university faculty, he pointed to Stanford's individualism, its serenity and lack of red tape, and its future as a place for scholars.

The quality of what they [the Founders] have given is unique in character. . . . The original foundation had something eccentric in it. Let Stanford not fear to be eccentric to the end, if need be. Let her not imitate; let her lead, not follow. . . . Not vast but intense; less a place for teaching youths and maidens than for training scholars; devoted to truth, radiating influence, setting standards . . . mediating between America and Asia, and helping the more intellectual men of both continents to understand each other.[4]

With two calamities behind it, the undaunted class of '06 faced brightly forward to Stanford's destiny and its own. But slightly more than a month after James's popular speech, the university's plans and hopes again were abruptly sidetracked. Early in the morning of April 18, 1906, Stanford was struck by the San Francisco earthquake. In the morning light, the Stanford community poured into the streets to survey the damage. Crowds wandered in silence to see the rubble of many of the largest and newest buildings. Wrote student Edith Mirrielees, "As the dust settled, ruin after ruin stood out in sharp relief against the blue of the early morning sky—the ragged outline of the Memorial Arch, the pile of broken stone which had been a chimney, farther off, the gaping front of the Chemistry building, and the big library dome towering up unsupported. The watchers in the street stood staring like people fascinated."[5]

Remarkably, there were only two fatalities at Stanford. One was a student, Junius Hanna, who was killed by a falling chimney in Encina Hall. The other was an employee in the campus powerhouse. As others fled, Otto Gerdes realized the danger of leaving the electricity on and returned to the powerhouse, which collapsed around him. His sacrifice was widely recognized by the community.

With mail service and the telegraph cut off and most trains canceled, Stanford was temporarily adrift. Jordan gave a rousing speech from the steps of Encina to bolster spirits. "It is not buildings that make a university," he proclaimed, "but professors and students, and I ask the students to demonstrate this." The crowd cheered and sang "Hail, Stanford, Hail."[6]

Cots, blankets, and tents were spread on the lawns in front of Encina and Roble and in front of houses for the first night, not so much because of damage but for fear of aftershocks. The community spent the second day clearing debris and salvaging belongings. Professors Harris J. Ryan and Rufus L. Green set off by car with more than 200 messages to find a working telegraph office. While many students sought to reassure worried parents, they had an even more immediate need. Banks would not cash checks, and transactions everywhere were on a cash-only basis. How could students buy food or get home? Most messages therefore were simple: "Am safe. Send fifty."

President Jordan, with typical optimism, at first predicted that classes would reconvene shortly. He quickly reconsidered and answered many of the questions pressing on the minds of the students. Classes were suspended, everyone would receive credit as though the year's work were completed, each professor was to be available to advise students, students entitled to degrees would be granted their diplomas, and the next term would open August 23. With academic business settled, many students went home or left for summer jobs.

Throughout those first two days, rumors had been flying: San Francisco was in ruins; Los Angeles was destroyed by a tidal wave; the insane at Agnews Asylum near San Jose were loose and running wild. Football heroes sat in front of Roble and various sororities with revolvers in their laps, ready to protect Stanford coeds from the bands of thugs rumored to be heading south from San Francisco to murder and loot.

The rumors about the destruction in San Francisco were largely correct. Following the earthquake, much of the central part of the city was engulfed in fire. Normally turned inward to its own problems and solutions, the Stanford community could hear the sound of dynamiting in the night air and could see a faint glow of the flames on the northern horizon. Students and faculty members went north to investigate, by train when it was running, by bicycle or walking if it was not. Many had relatives and friends in the city, many simply felt a need to help. At a mass meeting, volunteers were called together to help with the homeless, sick, and wounded of San Francisco. A Stanford relief corps headed north.

The Stanford headquarters was set up near the 25th and Guerrero streets train station. Armed with "student relief" passes, Stanford students explored the city and ended up helping at the other relief stations as well as distributing food and clothing. And when the Stanford relief crew needed relief, D. Charles Gardner, chaplain of Memorial Church, arrived with stove and cooking utensils. Appalled that the students subsisted on a sack of dirty dried prunes when they had time to eat at all, Gardner cooked by the curbside as long as Stanford students remained working at the station.

The earthquake left deep financial and physical wounds on the campus. Replacement cost of the lost campus buildings was estimated later that summer at more than three million dollars. In the aftermath, working students spent their summer sorting rubble, chipping mortar from bricks, serving as guards around roped-off buildings. With the consulting engineers' report in hand, the faculty reconstruction com-

mittee set to work finding workmen to carry out repairs. In spite of a local labor strike, the job was sufficiently completed in the two months available before fall registration. Since no books and little laboratory equipment had been lost, the academic function of the university was taken up in August where it left off.

The faculty trembled at the prospect of yet another "Stone Age." Would academic progress again be stymied as funds were diverted to ornamental architecture? Jordan wrote to colleague Andrew White at Cornell, "The Memorial Church, splendidly built but wrecked by the fall of its spire and flying buttresses, touches us deeply . . . but the new library, gymnasium and Museum annex, crushed like a pie set on edge, we have no feeling for. They have kept us impoverished for long, tedious years."[7]

In the battle of academic progress versus buildings, Jordan and the faculty ultimately won. Plans for rebuilding the gym, library, and museum annex were shelved. Memorial Arch disappeared forever. No significant new construction would be attempted for another decade.

In turn, in a sweeping change to the developing academic program, Stanford made its first major addition to the original Stanford trust in 1908 when it received the property and facilities of the Cooper Medical College of San Francisco.

Leland Stanford had assumed that a medical curriculum would one day be developed. In the Grant of Endowment he directed the trustees "to establish and have given at the University, by the ablest professors, courses of lectures upon the Science of Government, and upon Law, Medicine, Mechanics, and the other Arts and Sciences." On campus, professional educa-

tion was provided by departments of engineering, law, and education. But the acquisition of the Cooper Medical College as Stanford's fourth professional focus proved unpopular at a time when the university was recovering from the physical damage of the earthquake and experiencing a drop in the value of its original endowment. Many faculty and alumni were doubtful of the university's capacity to take on such an ambitious new program and feared its impact on other departments, particularly those in the humanities. But others felt that in order to develop Stanford's professional schools and research capacity, it must take a step outward to move forward.

The placement of a medical curriculum within a university structure was a late-nineteenth-century innovation. Earlier in the century, medical education was in the hands of commercial schools unaffiliated with colleges or universities. Founded by Dr. Samuel Elias Cooper as the first medical college on the Pacific Coast in 1858, the Cooper Medical College underwent a series of reorganizations, name changes, and affiliations to make ends meet. The College continued to operate with no salaried staff and a faculty of practicing physicians. All expenses had to be met by tuition. By the turn of the century, advances in medical science and the growing concern of the medical profession about standards necessitated more expensive laboratories and stringent control of curriculum. The Cooper Medical College, which required a high-school education only, could not raise the caliber of its work to meet this need without a significant increase in its endowment. Thus it began negotiations with Stanford and with the University of California for affiliation.

Many expressed doubt about whether San Fran-

cisco could support two university-level medical schools, that of Stanford and the Toland Medical College, already affiliated with the University of California. Representatives from the two universities met to negotiate for a union of the medical schools, but too many difficulties surfaced over unequal representation on the proposed governing board—California 5, Stanford 3. The two medical schools fell back on the traditional, and mutually beneficial, Stanford-California rivalry.

The opposition of the Stanford faculty, not so easily overcome, lasted into the next decade. One administration would seek to sever the university's relationship with the medical school, the next would knit the two strongly together. With a larger and larger percentage of the annual budget directed at the development of the new Stanford Medical School, a major change to the university's financial policy resulted—Stanford began to raise money. In its first financial campaign in 1912, the university let it be known that gifts would be welcome to improve hospital, clinical, and laboratory facilities, support professorships, build library collections, and develop the School of Nursing.

As the faculty and administration contemplated Stanford's academic future, student life continued at its own pace. Life was centered on campus. Automobiles were a rarity in the neighborhood—in fact, in the state, with only 800 vehicles registered in 1900. At the turn of the century, only one car had been allowed on campus by Mrs. Stanford in recognition of physician Ray Lyman Wilbur's need for quick access to his patients. Wilbur was required to keep the horseless carriage out of sight by driving around through College Terrace and up the Mayfield Road. After Mrs. Stanford's death in 1905, cars were permitted but discouraged, their routes restricted to a few campus roads and access via University Avenue (later renamed Palm Drive) absolutely forbidden. By 1906, there were six autos, three owned by faculty, three by students, and livery stables and bicycle shops far outnumbered shops dealing with the needs of the motorist.

The campus community relied largely on the livery stable "bus," bicycles, or walking to get to and from town until the trolley line from Palo Alto to the campus, the popular "Toonerville Trolley," was completed in 1909. For the trip up King's Mountain or to La Honda, a rented buggy or a "tally-ho," an open coach, was the thing.

San Jose, twenty miles to the south, became more attractive when the interurban transit line was completed through to San Jose in 1909; it had extended south from San Jose to the watering holes near Saratoga and Los Gatos in 1907. Hiking remained popular—in the hills, along Stevens Creek, or into the mountains behind Saratoga—as did trips out to the beaches at Santa Cruz and Capitola or up to Lick Observatory on Mount Hamilton. And when San Francisco, "The City," beckoned, with its Italian restaurants, opera, dances, and in time its silent-moving-picture houses, the students paid the price of a costly ticket on the Southern Pacific.

Stanford wins 13-8

Europe, even the East Coast of the United States, remained far away. "We were parochial," wrote Bruce Bliven, class of 1911 and renowned journalist:

Of the many world events during that decade, few reverberated more than faintly along the sandstone corridors beneath the red-tiled roofs. . . . True, the San Francisco earthquake and fire made a deep impression, because men were killed and buildings destroyed on campus. The voyage of the United States Fleet around the world a year later also bit in; we could and did go up to San Francisco to see the ships enter the unbridged Golden Gate. But other things seemed remote: Peary's discovery of the North Pole, Bleriot's first airplane flight across the English Channel, the dynamiting of the *Los Angeles Times*. Even great world events—the Italian-Turkish War, the Mexican Revolution against Diaz, the birth of the Chinese Republic—were hardly more than the hum of angry bees far off across a drowsy landscape.[8]

Yet, more focused on their surroundings than later generations, these students loved and appreciated the campus landscape. The Farm provided a remarkable sense of space and freedom of movement, an ambiance different from both the bustling cities of San Francisco and San Jose and the thriving farm towns, miles of rich orchards, vineyards, and nurseries of the "Valley of Heart's Delight."

Music and drama remained "grass roots." No music department or department of drama existed, and the Art Department was small and struggling. The church organist, the Stanford band, the Sophomore Farce, the

Junior Opera, the Senior Play were highly popular, as were visiting lecturers, musicians, and singers. The English Club was in full bloom, with its meetings an unpredictable array of discussion and argument, skits and readings. Its yearly productions could range from an outdoor drama in the arboretum to the publication of short stories or reminiscences of the university's first year.

The students were still overwhelmingly of middle- and lower-middle-class families, and the first generation of those families to attend college. Tuition was free to residents of California, except for a "syllabus fee" of several dollars. Students from out of state paid $30. Room and board in a nearby rooming house ran about $18 a month, and at "The Greek's" on University Avenue you could get a good three-course meal with beverage for 25 cents.

Traditions inherited from the "pioneer years" were well established. Freshmen still wore beanies and sophomores their porkpie hats, while the status of the junior was based on the condition of his top hat, or "plug," the more battered the better. The senior, matured beyond the scruffy life of the junior, sported the sedate field hat, or "senior sombrero." The yearly alfresco Junior Play scandalized and entertained.

Extracurricular activities—sports, drama, journalism, clubs—were solidly entrenched as a key part of Stanford life. Wrote Frank Hill of the class of 1911:

It was something in the pioneer tradition—an emphasis on individual effort and the individual's right to succeed on his own terms, a much larger amount of academic leeway than its great rival permitted, and an energy which sprang from the circumstances of its birth and its need to win success. . . . As a new student at Stanford I quickly understood what was expected of me. It was expected that I would enter into curricular and extracurricular life with zest—that anything I did (study, debating, writing, athletics) would be done vigorously and fully.[9]

The energy directed at class rivalries, and the subsequent level of violence, had also become entrenched. The Sophomore-Freshman Rush, the "lowest form of interclass activity," became a bloody affair as sophomores and freshmen clashed on the muddy football field, hoping to tie up as many members of the opposing class as possible and, when necessary, using sharp rocks and knives to get loose. The Junior-Senior Melee of the Plug Ugly lasted until abolished by the students in 1913. By then, the plug hat had lost its popularity, and the Plug Ugly play most of its audience.

Hazing took on a variety of forms, with "tubbing" the most popular. Unrepentant freshmen, or simply the unwary, might find themselves grabbed by upperclassmen and dumped head down in an Encina bathtub full of water. Once the bubbles stopped, presumably because breathing had stopped as well, the freshman was released.

Hazing, tie-ups, plug uglies, the violence in interclass rivalry, or the competition between "Frats" and "Roughs," were part of the male student's life.

Whether a sign of maturity or of the close attention of administration and faculty to the deportment of women, the Stanford coed maintained her reputation for responsible self-government, academic accomplishment, financial stability, and decorum. "No nice girl would have dreamt of smoking in public, and not one in a hundred did so privately; a maiden in my class, discovered in her room with an inexplicable lighted cigarette, had to talk very fast to avoid being suspended."[10]

Athletics for both sexes were, like all extracurricular activities, popular and vigorous. Football had replaced baseball in the hearts of the campus population, and educators across the country were surprised by its popularity—and growing commercialism—as a spectator sport. As was the custom, competitive athletics was in the hands of the Stanford student body. The ASSU hired the coaches, managed the teams, arranged the events, managed the gate receipts. But the balance of income to spending was precarious even if managed wisely. Famous name professional coaches, at substantial salaries, were lured to college campuses to swell the gate receipts. The ASSU was going broke, and the university was concerned about the number of serious injuries occurring at each game.

In an attempt to tone down the violence of American football, both Stanford and the University of California officially switched to rugby in 1906. After a number of years of relative calm, athletic relations between Stanford and the University of California became increasingly strained, but the Big Game continued unabated and the Stanford-California rivalry pervaded athletic, academic, and social life on campus.

The student body was largely unaware of the process of transition from the Jordan years to the presidency of John Casper Branner in 1913. After his retirement as president, Jordan remained a highly visible part of campus life, a symbol of the "Stanford spirit." Branner, long a part of the university administration as chair of the Geology Department and university vice president, served as president two brief years before retiring in 1916. Yet the events of the later Jordan and the Branner years would have repercussions for decades to come.

David Starr Jordan had become quintessentially identified with Stanford University. In his memoirs, Ray Lyman Wilbur remembered Jordan as a man of courage, wit, and initiative, "as far away as the Senator could wish from the run-of-the-mill college president of those days. . . . [He had] such an informal and striking way of talking that he quickly made a sensation in educational circles, particularly when he championed the student's right to choose his own course of study."[11]

Jordan's boundless enthusiasm and incorrigible optimism were contagious, and he drew to Stanford a student body and a faculty that appreciated freedom from the restraint of academic tradition and opportunity for independent thinking. He believed strongly in student honor and the capacity of the individual for self-discipline. Jordan's university would have no complicated rules of student discipline. The only laws would be those of the State of California. This philosophy had been formalized in 1896 in the publication of Stanford's Fundamental Standard:

In the government of the University the largest liberty consistent with good order is allowed. Students are expected to show both within and without the University such respect for order, morality and the rights of others as is demanded of good citizens. Failure to do this will be sufficient cause for removal from the University.[12]

Students, however, often remembered Jordan's more colorful interpretation. As he explained to one entering class: "The place is yours; it was made for you. The professors are here for you. The whole place is yours. . . . You are here to study, and we can ask you to go home if you don't do it." Those who did not wish to participate in the exciting work of the university—the unprepared, the idle, the vicious—would be taken to the edge of the campus and "dropped off."[13]

And dropped off he was (rarely was a woman expelled), often without recourse. Student discipline was in the hands of the faculty's Student Affairs Committee, the Academic Council's most unpopular and thankless committee assignment. The committee tended toward making an example of individual cases and stubbornness in reconsidering their verdicts. Without an avenue of appeal, but unwilling to take on collective accountability, the student body rallied periodically behind the individual sacrificed to principle.

The battles between the Student Affairs Committee and the student body—more specifically, student editors and inhabitants of the Encina "madhouse" and fraternities—became more frequent and heated until the "Liquor Rebellion" of 1908.

While the days of free handouts of wine at the Stanfords' winery on campus were long past, nearby Mayfield had offered the pioneer students the diversion of saloons and billiard halls in a rural setting otherwise limited in cultural distraction. The "Road to Mayfield" and the "Mayfield habit" became part of the standard Stanford vocabulary, and drinking central to the first decade's song and story.

But a movement in favor of prohibition had been

growing in California since the 1890's. Palo Alto was dry by city ordinance at the suggestion of Leland Stanford and was increasingly prosperous, attracting young families looking for quiet rural homes where they could raise families within commuting distance of San Francisco. Many of those families were associated with the university, and newspapers referred to the Stanford faculty's strong prohibitionist leanings. Yet in spite of this feeling, the university administration was not inclined to interfere in what it deemed the student's responsibility for self-discipline, even when San Francisco newspapers gleefully reported destructive student binges following intercollegiate events held in the City.

In 1903, the floundering town of Mayfield went dry

in a fleeting attempt to keep up with Palo Alto. Menlo Park's fourteen saloons took on the weight, and significant profit, of the student trade. "The Road to Mayfield" quickly became "The Road to Menlo," but the road was now a good two miles farther. Beer and whiskey made their way into Encina and the fraternity houses, and the "drunken habit" became a campus rather than neighborhood phenomenon.

By the time of the earthquake, a vocal minority was determined to make the Encina "beer bust" a Stanford tradition while fraternity rushing brought equally vocal binges along the fraternity row. Menlo Park residents complained of the increasing rowdyism of the students, of assaults and vandalism, and they were joined by faculty and student campus residents in pressing for an end to alcohol on campus.

The Student Affairs Committee was unable to deal effectively with the problem. When the Committee expelled two Encina undergraduates for sponsoring yet another beer bust the previous semester, 250 residents of Encina petitioned the university. They offered to give up hazing freshmen and to behave themselves if the university would recognize that the two students had reformed since the incident and had returned to the university, paying registration fees and rent. The committee refused to reconsider.

In Stanford's first major student demonstration against university policy, several hundred students loudly marched in protest across the campus and through the library. The Committee was appalled and

threatened to suspend or expel all who had participated.

In time, the liquor problem was quelled not by the
Student Affairs Committee but by the State of California and by the students themselves. In November
1907, student and faculty residents organized the
Campus Civic Federation to pressure the university
administration and, if necessary, the Board of Trustees
into taking a stand.

The lobbying of the Campus Civic Federation was
suddenly made easier by a fatal accident in Palo Alto
the next year. An undergraduate, returning drunk
from a Menlo Park saloon, mistakenly entered a house
in Palo Alto. Thought to be a burglar, he was shot to
death. Within a year, the State of California took action as the legislature forbade the sale of alcohol
within a mile and a half of the university.

This restriction in itself would have done little, simply pushing the available supply of alcohol yet a little
farther walking distance from Encina and fraternity
row. But by 1908, the students' definition of "student
control" was changing from that of freedom from faculty interference in matters of nonacademic conduct to
corporate responsibility. Although many students initially were reluctant to take on self-rule, the women
students acted first when the Women's Judicial Board
was empowered with the duties and responsibilities
for student discipline.

For the men, the role model was the Encina Club,
which first attempted to take on responsibility for Encina residents from the monitors and caretakers hired
by the university. A joint conference of Encina and
fraternity representatives led to a men's conference in
1907, modified a year later to consist of upperclassmen
selected for each department by students with declared majors.

The Men's Council was established as a judicial
body in 1912, aided by student advisors. The new post
of Dean of Women had proven a successful comple-
ment to the Women's Judicial Board, but many male
students were openly hostile to the Men's Council and
vehemently opposed to the creation of a Dean of Men.
Student advisors would suffice for the next few years,
their success due in part to the appointment of young
men like Almon Roth, class of '12, president of the
ASSU and an influential and wise student body
leader.

While student life had its element of violence, the
larger community as a whole sympathized with the
idealistic political leanings of David Starr Jordan. Jordan, joined by faculty colleagues, had been interested
in pacifism since the vocal reaction of a minority of
Americans against the Spanish-American War and
American occupation of the Philippines that resulted
in the foundation of the Anti-Imperialist League. In
1910, he was elected chief director of the World Peace
Foundation, and his only two sabbaticals from presidential duties were devoted to delivering antiwar addresses to audiences in Europe, Japan, and Korea in
1909 and 1910.

Rumors began to circulate that Jordan wished to re-
tire from the university in order to devote his full attention to the peace movement and the growing tur-
moil in Europe. When the rumors reached the University of California, President Benjamin Ide Wheeler
wrote Jordan:

I heard from a friend of yours that you had considered with-
drawing at some time during the coming year from the presidency of Stanford. Will you let me advise and urge against
this step. It is not the time. . . . There is no one in the State
whose word goes so far. They expect you and desire you to
set the standard for Stanford University and guarantee it to
them. . . . I hope you will stay with it, say five years more—
indeed, I shall be lonesome enough without you.[14]

Jordan decided to stay, dividing his time between
Stanford and the Foundation's activities, but was frustrated at the lack of time he had to devote to two jeal-
ous constituencies. Jordan's dilemma was solved by
another pacifist and Jordan admirer of the Pioneer
Class of 1895. Herbert Hoover had been elected to the
Board of Trustees in 1912, the second alumnus to
serve on the board. Hoover's energy, managerial skill,
and ambition for his alma mater took the trustees by
storm.

The Board had tended to resist changes and new
demands, to remain aloof from the everyday life and
activity of the campus, and to search for ways to econ-
omize on academic programs of little interest to the
San Francisco business community. Hoover prodded
and nudged the Board to review its conservative financial procedures (which had included keeping the
president in the dark about the financial status of the
university) and direct a larger portion of an unusually
large emergency fund toward immediate improvements in the academic program. Sympathetic to Jordan's predicament, Hoover also sensed that it was
time for a graceful change of leadership. With the
Board's approval, he offered Jordan a "chancellorship"
that would continue his connection to the university
but allow him more time for his other interests. In
1913, Jordan accepted, and his friend and vice president, John Casper Branner, was named president.

The Jordan era had not quite ended. The 63-year-
old Branner saw his role as one of place-keeping, providing a bridge between pioneer Stanford and the new
generation of leadership. He promised the university
two years until his well-deserved retirement sched-
uled for 1915. He successfully continued Jordan's
struggle for improved communication and interaction
among university administration, trustees, and faculty
and for support for student self-government. Branner
lobbied hard for his faculty and alumni, calling for improved salaries to attract and keep quality faculty and
for larger representation of alumni in trustee and university affairs. He brought attention back to the
beauty of the campus and to the aesthetic and emotional quality of the original quadrangle/arcade concept of the founders and their architects.

Most of Branner's efforts, in fact, were remarkably

successful, with one exception—the Stanford Medical School. "I know from what you wrote to me a while ago that you think the medical school a great acquisition," wrote Branner to Jordan shortly after becoming president. "But just the same it has the University around the neck, and we are all on the way to the bottom together."[15] He was shocked to find the Board considering discontinuing selected academic programs on campus, beginning with the Department of Art, in order to devote more general funding for the medical program. Branner strongly recommended, with faculty support, getting rid of the Medical School altogether.

But in this fight he was supported by neither Jordan nor Hoover. Both viewed the Medical School as Stanford's next step toward advanced university research while reemphasizing the practical contributions to society of university-sponsored professional education. In addition, Hoover's loyalty to his former major professor was overshadowed by his friendship with the Medical School's most ardent and effective spokesman, the new dean of medicine, Ray Lyman Wilbur. Not only did Jordan and Hoover support Wilbur's advocacy for increased funding for the new school, they recommended Wilbur's nomination as the next president of Stanford University.

Reaction on campus to the nomination of the outspoken Wilbur was mixed. Some, including Branner, pressed for alternate candidates; at one point Branner recommended a professor of classics from Princeton. But, wrote Jordan to Branner, Leland Stanford would "turn over in his grave" if he knew that a "professor of classics from the most reactionary university in America" were to become president.[16]

However, torn by the medical school–campus competition, the alumni and faculty also were extremely anxious over the selection of a president familiar with Stanford's ideals and style. They wanted someone shaped by Stanford training and able to guide and develop the university in its own way, not one imitative of any other institution. Wilbur was, indeed, the new quintessential Stanford man. Member of the "almost pioneer class" of 1896 and graduate of the Cooper Medical College, professor and dean of medicine, campus physician and active alumni leader, he was intimately familiar with the university's problems and possibilities. His personality and philosophy would shape Stanford life for more than a quarter century, from one war to another, through rampant inflation and debilitating depression.

A picture of serenity greeted the "Calamity Class" of 1906—view from Memorial Church north to Memorial Arch around 1903.

Jane Stanford in her favorite lace and pearls sits for her last portrait before her death in 1905. Mrs. Stanford left the university with its second major building program virtually completed and with total control of its $20 million endowment, one of the largest in the country.

The largest crowd in campus history attended Mrs. Stanford's funeral in Memorial Church, then proceeded to the family mausoleum in the arboretum.

A frieze surmounting Memorial Arch included Jane and Leland Stanford on horseback and a Central Pacific locomotive in its depiction of "The Progress of Civilization in America."

Just fourteen months after Mrs. Stanford's death, her beloved church and Memorial Arch were ruined in the great earthquake of April 1906. The church steeple collapsed, blowing outward the huge mosaic scene on the facade. The exquisite interior mosaics were largely undamaged but could not be saved when the church later was rebuilt around a new structural frame.

One unlucky Encina student, Junius Hanna, was carried to his death by a falling chimney, one of two fatalities at Stanford.

Damage, estimated at nearly $2 million, included destruction of the new library and gymnasium, seen beyond the debris of the east arcade, and of the new Palm Drive entrance gates.

Encina men gathered on the morning of the quake to hear President David Starr Jordan's reassurances after a horse-drawn ambulance carried away the few injured.

When the marble statue of Louis Agassiz was found headfirst through the concrete sidewalk, one professor quipped: "He was great in the abstract, but not in the concrete."

For the next few days, the community slept outside, prompted as much by rumors of devastating aftershocks as by structural damage: camping along the row and in front of Encina.

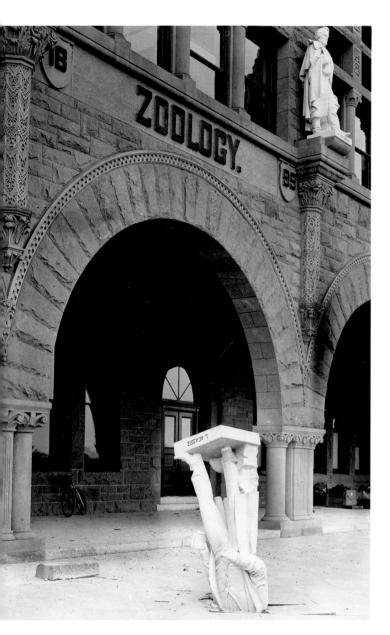

Chi Psi members, their house pitched off its foundations, used humor to ease the tension.

"It is not buildings that make a university but professors and students," Jordan told the community in 1906: chemistry faculty and graduate students in 1907 and three of the original faculty (left to right), Oliver P. Jenkins, Clara Stoltenberg, and Frank M. McFarland.

The faculty's board-and-batten clubhouse, hidden in the arboretum, was used until a new club was built in 1965 off Lagunita Drive.

Classics professor Ernest Whitney Martin also directed the Stanford band. Psychologist Lillien Martin (no relation) originally a physicist, joined the faculty in 1899, following study and research in Germany.

"You are here to fit yourselves for useful careers,"
Leland Stanford told stu-
dents opening day: nursing
students at Stanford's
newly acquired medical college in San Francisco; a
Hopkins Marine Station
1906 lab class; advanced entomology on campus in
1911.

Geology seniors of the "Calamity Class" of '06 sport-
ing their senior sombreros
and displaying the latest,
and earliest, tools of their
trade.

Faculty and students who
joined in serious discus-
sions of world political issues in the Cosmopolitan
Club here surround the university's revered president
and honorary member.

Theodore Roosevelt tours campus with the Jordan family and John Casper Branner in 1911 after his lecture telling Stanford students they must have more than expert technical training.

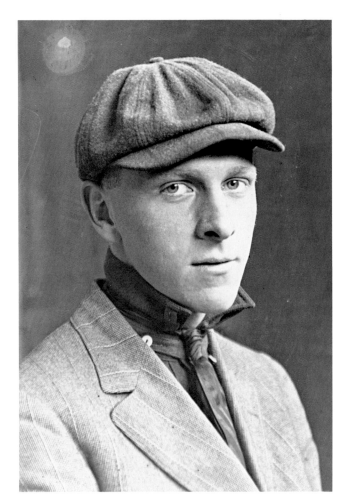

Formal poses by Stanford's informal students: Earle Knight, '14, and Irene Rowlands, '13.

Student albums included an increasing number of candid shots captured with the hand-held camera—like the one clutched by a young student.

George Casper Branner (seated at left, with a friend), son of the geologist, was a meticulous album keeper.

1913

Ruled only by a fundamental standard and commonly held sense of propriety, Jordan's students shared a strong sense of community.

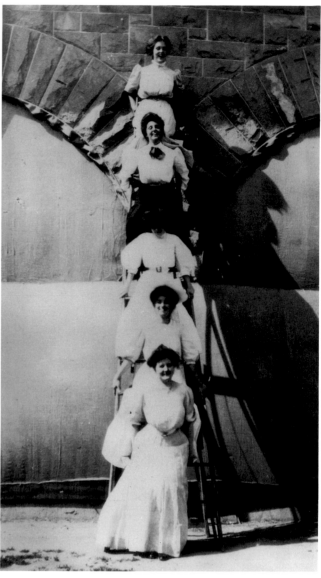

The camera of an unknown Roble Hall resident captures spoofing "early (?) in the evening at Maxim's."

Roughs of the "Brotherhood of Engineers" have their day, near the engineering labs, in 1912.

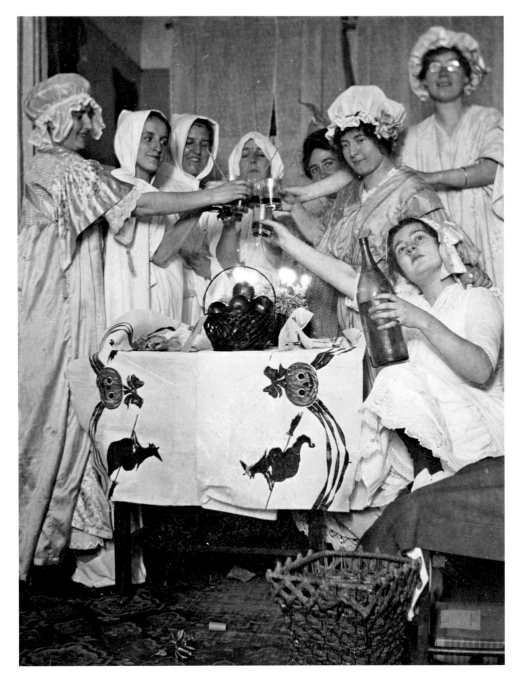

Hamming it up for the camera during a Halloween party in Roble.

Good-natured conviviality developed into a serious drinking problem on campus as Mayfield went dry and beer became more prevalent in Encina and along the Row.

"After hours at Stanford" often meant a trip to a local saloon.

Although he was called "the Hermit," Domingo Grosso (opposite) enjoyed visitors to his Jasper Ridge mining camp, welcoming them with homemade wine.

The heyday of initiations turned from hazing into the more creative brand of Stanford satire. Honor society Skull and Snakes initiates capture campus attention as they campaign "suffragette style." Another group rolls peanuts the hard way.

Initiates to Phi Delta Phi and the Press Club (far right) stage plays with murder, mayhem, and all-around joshing near the Quad and on the Post Office steps.

#5617
The Plug Ugly Fight.

The year 1913 saw the last official Plug Ugly before the University Conference banned the annual confrontation between juniors and seniors. The justification: the Plug Ugly play was no longer funny, juniors no longer routinely wore the plug, and the half-hour scramble on the Quad had become too violent.

Personification of the freshman-sophomore rivalry remained healthy, and physical, in the Frosh-Soph Tie-Up. Freshmen march to the football field as sophomores gather behind Encina Hall. Seniors monitor the Frosh-Soph battle, egg on underclassmen, and tally the trussed bodies for the final score.

How they loved parades: men of the Row stage a Washington Day Parade, complete with costumes, stunts, and skits.

More parades and minimal class attendance: students supply their own circus parade; two others bicycle through "Yurup" during Junior Week celebration.

Junior class festivities, which had lasted a day in 1894, stretched to almost a week by 1915 and encompassed every excuse for costume, including the briefest.

Junior Week's long-held tradition, the water carnival at Lagunita.

Senior Week, too, included parades, concessions, and the formal senior ball.

Drama at Stanford played outside as often as in: the chorus line, Stanford style; Robin Hood, staged in the arboretum by the English Club; drumming up business for Gilbert and Sullivan's "Iolanthe."

Ram's Head, then an all-male drama club, never hesitated to include female roles as the ratio of women to men students on campus fell to 1–4. William "Boomer" Forbes, at left, and Dick Morgan as dancing girls in the 1912 production "Rambling Rameses."

The 1913 varsity rugby team. Fast moving rugby replaced American football at Stanford as the "cleaner, more democratic" game from 1906 through the First World War.

The week before Big Game soon included key ingredients: the bonfire, more ambitious every year as each freshman class vied for the biggest pyre, and the rally in Assembly Hall.

"Rooter stunts" began in 1904 with hats. Soon copied by the other side during the Big Game, these were followed by a succession of Stanford innovations, including card stunts, confetti, pigeons with streamers, and megaphones.

The 1912 Big Game became a mudfight within minutes.

The new Encina Gymnasium replaced the 25-year-old wooden men's gym in 1915.

The Stanford track team of 1908 poses at Oakland's ferry landing on its way to the Western Conference track meet in Chicago. Coach E. W. "Dad" Moulton is third from right.

After a slow start during the 1890's, Stanford's track and field program was turned around by E. W. "Dad" Moulton, coach and trainer from 1902 to 1914; his 1904 team included Norman Dole, whose record in the pole vault was the first world mark set by a Stanford athlete.

The Track House, here at the start of a mile race at Angell Field, was refurbished as a sports shop in 1986.

The "Stanford rooting section," including Professor Charles "Daddy" Marx, was small but enthusiastic at the 1915 Poughkeepsie Regatta. They cheered a team that "didn't stand a chance" but barely lost first place to Cornell.

The 1915 varsity crew warms up on the Oakland estuary before a race with Washington and California. Crew flourished from 1904 to 1920 despite little financial support.

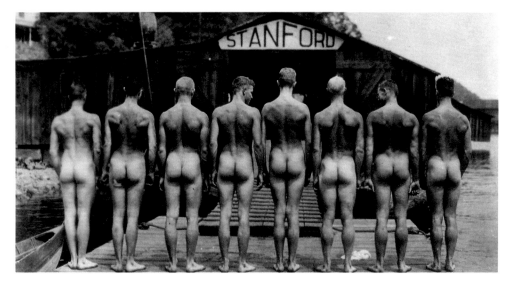

Class of 1916 crew team bares all at Stanford's Redwood Slough boat house.

The informality of the '04 alumni team, lounging on the steps of Stanford Inn, belies the seriousness of Stanford baseball. Public popularity of collegiate baseball was at a peak. The varsity team of 1913, posing in their scroll "S" uniforms, played three games a week.

Professor Clelia D. Mosher, a vocal advocate of women's competitive athletics, stressed exercise and loose clothing in everyday life.

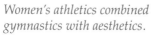

Women's athletics combined gymnastics with aesthetics.

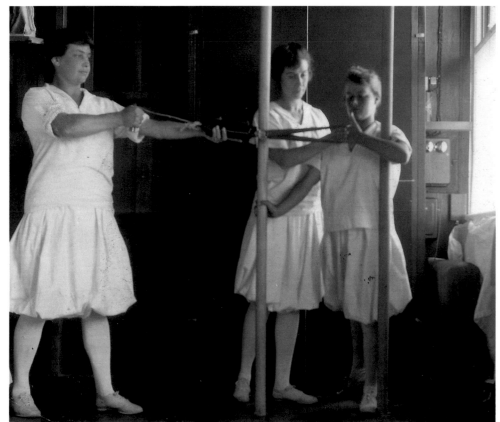

Students measure wrist power for Mosher's study on the muscular strength of women.

John Caspar Branner, caught in a candid snapshot as he walks with Board of Trustees president Timothy Hopkins to his investiture as Stanford's second president, 1913.

Marching to the 1915 commencement, held in Memorial Church. Caps and gowns had been worn at the ceremonies since 1899.

The Farm at the end of an era: the footbridge across San Francisquito Creek was little changed since Stock Farm days, but "gas buggies" now parked in front of Encina Hall.

By 1913, Sand Hill Road showed more tire marks than wagon ruts as it wound into the foothills.

Tightening the Reins, 1916-1929

A student's principal business is his study.

RAY LYMAN WILBUR, *August 5, 1916*

By 1916, Europe was caught in a war that would bring profound changes to its social, political, and economic structure. At Stanford University, major changes—albeit less devastating ones—also were underway. With Ray Lyman Wilbur's inauguration that year, the future of Stanford students, faculty, administration, and Board of Trustees was in new hands. Not imported from another state nor another college, these were alumni hands, attracted by the Stanford family's practicality, trained by the old guard, and nurtured on Jordan's optimism. The university approached its second quarter century with renewed energy but a new passion for order in a drive for accountability and discipline.

This new approach was personified by its new president, Dr. Ray Lyman Wilbur. Wilbur would represent an administrative style that both inspired and infuriated Stanford students, that both puzzled and intrigued faculty and alumni.

Wilbur's style had been recognized, and somewhat feared, by the older faculty and trustees before his inauguration. It did not take the student body long to recognize that the first cycle of Stanford's development was over and a new era begun. In an editorial directed at the first freshman class to know only Wilbur's administration, the editor of the newly born student publication *The Stanford Illustrated Review*, a senior, wrote: "All of you won't like him. Not all of us older ones have grown up enough to like him. But you'll see action under him and you won't forget that Ray Lyman Wilbur, Stanford '96, is the administrator of the University."[1]

Wilbur made it clear as early as his first address to the student body on the day before his inauguration that he intended to wean the students of the trivialities that had come to be associated with undergraduate college life. In his autobiography, he later explained, "The situation at Stanford was such that young people could be very content to do a minimum amount of work and a maximum of play. Stanford's inviting climate for outdoor activities may have had something to do with it, but there was a general trend over the whole country to overemphasize the social aspects, the side shows, of college life."[2]

Wilbur's concern for improving the level of undergraduate scholarship was part of a wave of reform of higher education spreading across the country. Like

Woodrow Wilson, president of Princeton University, and Harvard president A. Lawrence Lowell, Wilbur was convinced that the energy and spirit directed at play could be redirected towards study.

Midway through his first year, Wilbur made his expectations clear to parents of Stanford students and prospective students in a letter that would be long remembered. In August 1916 he made "a few practical suggestions." The Stanfords, he pointed out, had not intended to provide a fashionable educational veneer for the ornamentation of idle and purposeless lives.

A student's principal business is his study. He needs enough money to buy food, lodging, simple clothes, books, stamps, and the like and to pay certain fees and dues, admission to a few entertainments, and special dental and medical bills. Any money supplied beyond these simple needs means that time will be wasted in spending it. . . . It takes time to run an automobile, and it often leads to life off the campus, to extravagance and much foolishness. There is plenty to do in the way of variety right at the University, with its swimming pools, athletic fields, gymnasia, beautiful walks, and the like. There is no need to go to San Francisco more than once or twice a semester, and the trip can be conveniently and cheaply made by train. . . . The student who is not content to lead the simple, clean, industrious life expected on the Stanford campus should go elsewhere.[3]

A month later, Wilbur took aim at fraternities. Fraternities and sororities had established themselves early in Stanford's history, providing much-needed room and board without expense to the university's fragile endowment. By 1916, twice as many Stanford students lived in fraternities and sororities as in dormitories and off-campus housing. While its nine sorority chapters, for the most part, maintained high scholarship records, members of Stanford's 24 fraternities were consistently in the bottom third of the scholarship lists, accompanied by the varsity football and baseball teams. Chapter houses were falling into disrepair, and the university received regular complaints from local merchants about bills long overdue. Wilbur put the students on notice.

The former Encina resident did not want to abolish fraternities but insisted they become a more constructive part of university life at Stanford. Scholarship and discipline problems, combined with the failure to meet financial obligations, meant the fraternities were "a disintegrating influence [and] that membership is not advantageous to the student." Wilbur gave the individual chapters two years to bring up their scholarship record and pay their bills, or he would work to disband those that failed. And, to discourage the growing sense of elitism on campus, he would impose a rule that all freshmen men must live in dormitory housing, as soon as adequate space was available.[4]

Wilbur's inaugural year was dubbed the "year of changes" as anxiety grew regarding the administration's alarming review of all things academic, structural, and social. But behind it all, even more alarming, loomed the war in Europe. The university community was swept first into humanitarian efforts, then military preparedness, and ultimately participation in the American war effort.

David Starr Jordan had warned of the impending violence long before war broke out in 1914, but the growing tension in Europe had remained little more than the topic of abstract discussions among faculty and debate competitions among students. In the fall of 1914 Herbert and Lou Henry Hoover brought the war home to the campus with their highly personalized campaign for Belgian famine relief. The fundraising campaign was a national one, but the Hoovers expected, and received, a special response from their alma mater. On visits from Europe, the Hoovers captured the imagination of the campus—and captured a number of Stanford faculty who were given leaves of absence to join other alumni in Europe in taking leading roles in the voluntary northern European relief effort. While the war remained a European one, faculty families and student groups organized fetes and fairs, gathered donations of money, and made up shipments of relief supplies. Reports on the status of the national relief effort, and especially Stanford's contribution to the campaign for funds and supplies, appeared regularly in alumni and student publications over the next several years.

Since 1914, foreign-born students and faculty had returned home to enlist, and a few American students were enticed by the romanticism of the war overseas to join foreign ambulance and flying corps. Nonetheless, the Stanford community was stunned by news of its first two casualties at the front, James Grant Fergusson '08 and Robert Edouard Pellissier, assistant professor of Romance languages, both killed in France in the summer of 1916. News of the deaths of Pellissier and Fergusson inspired yet another fund-raising drive, this time to erect plaques in their memory in Memorial Court and to present a fully equipped ambulance to the second Stanford ambulance unit.

Even at the front, Stanford's untiring competition with the University of California persisted. Following America's entry into the war in April 1917, Stanford and Cal each had assembled an ambulance corps equipped with American flag to present to the French commander. They raced across the Atlantic to be the first to the front. Stanford won and returned its flag, adorned with the Croix de Guerre, to stand posted in Memorial Church until the late 1960's.

Just as Americans across the country were grappling with their reactions to the European war, the Stanford community became increasingly torn between the emotional appeal of Jordan's pacifist ideals and the need for humanistic support of those suffering in the conflict on the one side, and Wilbur's vocal support of military preparedness and the growing inclination toward more active participation in the war effort on the other. Faculty were encouraged to take leaves of absence for Red Cross work, for famine relief in northern Europe and the Near East, or for participation in activities of the World Court, and funds were raised to send yet more student ambulance teams to the front. In addition, the Reserve Officers Training Corps was in full swing by the fall of 1916. Among the students in particular, preparedness was winning popularity over "peace at any price."

Throughout 1916, Americans remained undecided about intervention, but popular sentiment became increasingly anti-German. When the United States entered the war in April 1917, Stanford University came under attack. Jordan's reputedly pacifist campus was accused of harboring faculty who promoted "peace at any cost," faculty who had attended universities in Germany and who, therefore, must have German sympathies. Stanford was, in fact, modeled on the German research university, and it continued to teach German literature and language. Even its motto, "Die Luft der Freiheit weht," was, quite uncommonly, in German rather than Latin. Critics questioned Stanford's loyalty and its place as a viable institution of higher learning for the youth of America. Faculty found themselves individually and collectively attacked in the press, from lecture audiences, and by parents.

In 1914, Jordan's popular talk "Confessions of a Peace-maker" had drawn large audiences. By 1916, he was jeered and threatened. That year the Board decided not to renew Jordan's three-year term as chancellor and ended his formal relationship with Stanford's faculty and administration. To what extent Stanford's Board of Trustees had been swayed by popular opinion is difficult now to document.

Despite the loss of his valued chancellorship, Jordan continued to speak out for world peace until Congress declared war in April 1917. In a statement issued to the press, the unrepentant Jordan then declared, "I would not change one word I have spoken against war. But the issues are now changed. At home and abroad the first question is now the worldwide defense of government by the people and for the people."[5]

Wilbur, who had received a death threat the previous year because of his vocal support for military preparedness, now took pains to point out to critics that *his* Stanford had already made many contributions to the war effort. In addition to long-term support of the Belgian relief campaign and five ambulance corps units, it could boast of an ROTC program among the top ten in the country and of an intensive military course of drill and instruction for 850 male students. Stanford also offered the use of its laboratories and the services of its hospital and staff to the

provided medical, social, and recreational support for Camp Fremont, newly established in Menlo Park by the Army.

Stanford women were not enrolled in university military service but volunteered for active duty in other war activities. Eighteen women, led by English professor Edith Mirrielees, were supported by a highly successful fund-raising drive. They left for France in August 1917 as the "Stanford Women's Unit for Relief Work in France" and served with the Red Cross. Professor Clelia Mosher surveyed conditions for the relief of war orphans and refugee children. Others enlisted as nurses in the Army, Navy, and British hospital services, worked locally with the Red Cross and other agencies, and organized food and supplies for the continuing relief effort.

The war also gave Stanford women a special opportunity on campus. Women students now outnumbered men, and they enthusiastically took on many positions of student power that the men had previously monopolized. As at most American universities, student political power emerged not only from the elected officers of the student body but from those in key positions on student publications and in important clubs. With the men gone, women moved out of the realm of society reporters and into the ranks of news reporters for *Stanford Daily*. By 1918, over half of the reporters were women, and a few, like Ruth Taylor and Dorothy Driscoll, tasted student power in the formerly male-dominated roles of news editor and managing editor. The war soon ended and both the men and the tradition of a separate "woman's editor" returned, but the precedent had been set.

Those who came back to the campus in 1919 would see change most apparent in the look of the place: the campus was undergoing a face-lift. A new Roble Hall was completed in 1918, and additions were made to Encina Hall. A special art gallery was built with funds provided by Senator Stanford's youngest brother, Thomas Welton Stanford, to display his gift of Australian art. Plans for a new main library were well under way to replace the desperately overcrowded library in the Outer Quad with a new building next to the art gallery. The new library and art gallery were to form the corner of a new eastern quadrangle. The old li-

U.S. government. The 1917–18 and 1918–19 school years were dominated by the war. Commencement in the spring of 1917 saw graduating men in uniform for the first time and the presentation of an American flag to the third Stanford Ambulance Unit. Even the festivities of Senior Week 1918 "symbolized the war spirit" with "simple but fittingly patriotic" activities. The class of '19 *Quad*, published in mid-1918, portrayed an honor roll of twenty killed in action. Nor did the editors forget the many in uniform who died of the Spanish influenza epidemic before they had the chance to leave California.

Encina and Sequoia halls were turned over to the Army for use as barracks, and a temporary mess hall for 1,200 was built near the site of today's Meyer Library. The athletics program was operated by the Student Army Training Corps, and intercollegiate sports competitions were discontinued. Most social events were suspended unless they supported the war effort, such as the work of campus Red Cross. Volunteers

brary space in the Outer Quadrangle would be remodeled as a new administration building, and the humanities departments shifted around the Quad. Nor did Wilbur forget his colleagues at the Medical School—construction was under way on a new Stanford Hospital next to the Lane Hospital in San Francisco.

For the first time, the university provided a home for its president, an imposing mansion on "The Knoll," landscaped by John McLaren, the innovative designer of San Francisco's Golden Gate Park. And Stanford's favorite son, trustee Herbert Hoover, and his wife, Lou Henry Hoover, began construction of their new home on San Juan Hill.

By 1920, those few faculty from the old guard as yet unretired would find it difficult to recognize the academic program. In the fall of 1917, Stanford moved from the semester to the quarter system to make more efficient use of time and facilities, following the lead of the University of Chicago. School was now in session for four quarters over eleven months rather than nine, and students could select which quarter, if any, to take off for full-time work, field work, or vacation. Students now also could graduate at the end of any quarter once the required number of units had been earned.

Rescheduling had a minor impact compared to three changes in academic program: the elimination of the major professor system, the establishment of lower- and upper-division courses of undergraduate study, and the institution of a universitywide course requirement beyond the required proficiency in English.

The major professor system had been Stanford's dominant contribution to the late-nineteenth-century reform of American higher education. It was Jordan's method of emphasizing the influence of the faculty and encouraging specialization more typical of a university than of a small college. The student's course of study was directed by a chosen faculty advisor, or "major professor." All course work was elective, each course selected according to the student's interests and career goals rather than by participation in a collegewide course of required study. The system provided those unsure of their future careers with enormous freedom to explore a variety of courses, yet suited the need for the earliest and narrowest possible specialization by those students set on following a chosen career path. By 1919, critics outnumbered proponents as the national concern for the quality of scholarship and curriculum focused on transgressions rather than freedoms of elective coursework.

The faculty committee undertaking review of the system found itself reviewing the status of undergraduate education as well as relations among the 26 independent departments, each of which set curricular requirements and granted degrees. The committee found that departments required as many courses of their own as possible, discouraging nonspecialization even among freshmen. Technical departments were especially guilty of dissuading students from taking any courses, including science courses, outside their field.

As a result of the committee's work, the Academic Council established the Lower Division curriculum in 1920. The ingredients were basic: the first 90 units must include some training in a laboratory science, some proficiency in the English language, some acquaintance with a language other than the native, and some knowledge of history, social programs, and the duties of citizenship. A special faculty committee was formed to serve as advisors, and special courses were established in general biological and physical sciences for nonmajors.

The reform also created in 1923 the first course required of all freshmen, "Problems of Citizenship," designed "to examine the fundamental political, social and economic problems of the American people"; this universitywide requirement would evolve over the next five decades to encompass first historical, then cultural aspects of Western civilization.[6]

In its final break with the pioneer past, the academic program saw its most controversial change in the introduction of tuition fees for undergraduates in January 1920. Students, and their parents, were astonished to find themselves charged $40 per quarter, and within two years $75, at this reputedly less expensive university.

Leland Stanford had, in fact, predicted the need for tuition in the university's future. To an early inquiry from a *San Francisco Bulletin* reporter in 1889 about tuition, Stanford stated, "I do not believe anyone should have something for nothing. It is one of the first objects of the school to teach that labor is respectable and honorable, and that idleness is not."[7] But acknowledging the importance of a low-cost education for the working class, he trimmed the university program to enable it to open tuition-free in 1891.

Soon thereafter, however, the Trustees had found it necessary to charge incidental fees to cover expenses during the financial crisis of 1893. Various minor fees, including registration fees, laboratory and book fees, and fees for special student status, had mounted up over time; law and medical students had paid tuition since 1908. Now the university looked to tuition to cure a variety of ills—the deficit that had become an annual problem, inadequate student housing, loans needed by faculty, and inadequate faculty salaries and retirement benefits. Never one to avoid confrontation, Wilbur was quick to point out to students and outraged parents that tuition covered only about one-third of the cost of education for each student. He found it difficult, he added, to tell a faculty member who could only afford a bicycle to teach for free students who were coming to campus with their own cars.

As the 1920's progressed, the composition of the student body changed as it swung from a balance of working-class and middle-class students toward the solid middle and upper-middle classes. Offers of tuition loans and urgent pleas for increased scholarship funds did little to change the trend as the number of

working students who "earned while they learned" dropped yearly.

Also changing was the size of the student body; by 1921 it had more than quintupled the size at the university's opening 30 years before. During the next decade it would almost double again, growing from 2,882 students in 1919 to 4,633 ten years later. As Jordan had hoped to see, the percentage of graduate students also was increasing yearly, from 16 percent of total enrollment in 1919 to 33 percent by 1929. But in spite of the growth in the number of graduate students, the 1920's saw a growing presence of "college life" in American culture, centering on the customs, attitudes, competitions, and pranks of the stereotypical undergraduate. Jordan, and later Wilbur, had attempted unsuccessfully to bolster the university orientation toward graduate study and research by eliminating the freshman and sophomore, or "college," years of study from Stanford. Each was forced, in turn, to recognize that Stanford was firmly established as a four-year undergraduate institution, with entrenched traditions of college life. The president might have an impact on the variety and level of frivolity of college traditions, but the players would largely remain the same until well into the 1940's.

While the 1920's roared, however, student discipline matured at Stanford from the controversial efforts of the Committee on Student Affairs, once known as the "faculty fire-brigade," to a system of self-discipline through student representatives. Men's and Women's Councils, reorganized in 1916 and responsible to the president rather than the faculty, sat in judgment and set penalties for everything from violations of the Fundamental Standard to traffic infractions. Faculty influence on student behavior now centered on policy recommendations to the student councils and to the increasingly influential Dean of Men and Dean of Women. In 1921, an important innovation in disciplinary policy was presented by the students in petition to the Academic Council. With the adoption of the Stanford Honor Code that year, responsibility for honesty and integrity in the conduct of examinations was transferred from the faculty to the student body.

The students finally seemed in charge of their own affairs, but their empowerment was, in fact, circumscribed by the more active role of university administration. Jordan had placed his faith in the moral influence of great men and women of the faculty; by the 1920's, the university put its faith in constructive intervention and in role models of administrators like George Culver, Dean of Men, and Mary Yost, Dean of Women. Both wielded an especially strong influence on student attitudes and behavior, a role once envisioned as solely a faculty responsibility.

The code of behavior itself had not changed dramatically since Mrs. Stanford's era, but was more stringently documented and consistently regulated. The coed of the 1920's was no less responsible for balancing the complexities of social reputation with the rigors of academics. Yet unlike her pioneer sister, the Stanford woman now added into the balance wider opportunities, more relaxed relationships with Stanford men, and the new freedom presented by the automobile. In spite of invective against cars on campus, the automobile had become a common sight and a campus status symbol. The rugged hikes into the foothills enjoyed by turn-of-the-century students were replaced more often by dates to San Francisco or San Jose or excursions out to one of the beaches. And the wider the range of possibilities for getting away from the campus, and from university control, the more stringent grew regulations regarding curfews at women's residences, standards for acceptable behavior, and, for the first time, dress codes.

Wilbur's war against the "side shows" of campus life in time brought under direct administrative control key areas of student life—living groups, student discipline, scholarship. Not surprisingly, athletics soon came under scrutiny as well as the university turned to the nationwide debate over the role of intercollegiate athletics in American academic life.

Since the turn of the century, educators had debated the role of intercollegiate sports, particularly football, in higher education. Detractors pointed to the growing professionalism of athletes, to betting scandals and payoffs, and to coaches indifferent to the scholastic responsibilities of students and faculty. Reformers were also concerned about the growing number of injuries, many fatal, resulting from insufficient protection and from the warlike "anything for a victory" mentality. Faculty and administrators at some colleges succeeded in discontinuing sports competition altogether as unnecessary and distracting to the academic program.

But Americans were captivated by the color and drama of collegiate sports, brought to them now by radio and a nationwide news media. Athletics brought a new attention to higher education and encouraged alumni interest. Many university administrators deplored the excesses of football but promoted the traditional view that sports played a valuable role in building character. For the men, they pointed out, it was a training ground for the competition of business life. Even the far more limited sports for women promoted good health, self-confidence, and teamwork.

With its temperate climate and rural orientation, Stanford life from the beginning had included all levels of sports and outdoor life. Its reforming president found this neither distasteful nor discordant—he had followed Stanford teams enthusiastically since his undergraduate days. Instead, he saw in college sports a useful energy that could be harnessed for the good of the campus.

Although the university maintained some athletic facilities for the sake of health and recreation, competitive sports—including most intercollegiate games—continued to be organized and managed by the ASSU and other student organizations. Major team sports, particularly football, had become big business. Gate receipts from the Big Game with the University of Cal-

ifornia's varsity football team supported many other Stanford sports until the next season's Big Game. But professional coaches with "big-name" drawing power demanded increasingly larger salaries. Facilities were difficult to maintain, and travel to campuses of increasingly distant opponents was expensive. The ASSU was virtually bankrupt, overwhelmed by its athletic program and plagued by financial irresponsibility.

And when Wilbur entered office, athletic relations with the University of California were at an all-time low. Already in disagreement over the choice of rugby over American football as the primary football sport, the two student bodies vehemently disagreed about eligibility and hurled accusations of unsportsmanlike behavior. Following a dramatic public debate and student demonstrations, the Stanford students broke off athletic relations with California in 1915, while alumni shook their heads at the impending financial crisis posed by the loss of the lucrative Stanford-California games. A spirit of reconciliation would return only after a three-year break and three seasons of financially disappointing alternative Big Games for both campuses, and with Stanford's willingness to return to American football.

The controversy drew attention to Stanford's floundering athletic program and led to the establishment of one of Wilbur's most successful "control boards." The Board of Athletic Control, created in 1916, was made up of representatives of the student body, alumni, faculty, and administration. But student, faculty, and alumni representation changed often; it would be the administration that would maintain a continued influence through its representative, J. Pearce Mitchell. The influential Mitchell, University Registrar and Academic Secretary, served as the Board's treasurer (1917–43) and secretary (1920–43).

The Board took over management of all teams and facilities to create a self-supporting athletic program for the next two and a half decades—it would not be until after World War II that departments of Men's Athletics and Women's Athletics would take charge. The Board, rather than the students, employed Stan-

ford's talented coaches—among them Harry Maloney, Ernie Brandsten, Dink Templeton, and, in 1924, Glenn "Pop" Warner—who in turn developed strong, winning teams.

And the Board used innovative financing and strict accountability to build a series of new sports facilities that would remain at the center of the athletic program for the next 50 years: the Stanford Stadium (1922), the Basketball Pavilion (1922), the Sunken Diamond (1925), additions to Encina Gym and pool complex (1917, 1925), Roble Gym and pool (1931), the golf course (1930), and Angell Field (1933).

Accompanying the athletic building boom was the enormous increase in dormitory housing. The "New Roble" Hall provided many more rooms and improved facilities for the women while allowing the university to renovate "Old Roble," renamed Sequoia Hall, for men. Early in the decade, work was completed on the third building of the Stanford Union, aimed at providing dormitory and dining facilities for more Stanford women. For the men, Toyon (1923) and Branner (1924) followed after additions were made to Encina Hall. All undergraduates were now required, as Wilbur had proposed, to live in dormitories for their freshman year on the assumption that each student would benefit from at least one year in the more "democratic" atmosphere of the dorm before being rushed to the fraternity or sorority.

The women of the dormitories, sororities, and boarding houses joined a "Stanford 500" now noticeably in the minority. The 500 limitation had had little effect at Stanford until the number of women had actually reached 500 in 1904. But during the 1920's women rushed to colleges across the country, and the national average for undergraduate enrollment was almost 50 percent women. At Stanford, more than five women were applying for each available space; a small but steady proportion of spaces was reserved for the children of faculty and alumni.

The 1920's also saw a change of outlook in the average Stanford woman. Although entering with more impressive academic credentials than her predecessor in the pioneer class, she was less intent on training herself for a career and more likely to marry shortly after she graduated. Her friends came from a wider geographic range but, with ever increasing tuition, from more consistently affluent backgrounds. This was the peak decade of the sorority in American college life, and social functions—and their meanings—weighed heavily in determining a successful college career.

The limitation of enrollment of all undergraduates was an old temptation, first suggested by Jane Stanford, but initially applied only to women. Jordan had suggested channeling all freshmen and sophomores to state "junior colleges" that would teach lower-division work only, but as yet California had no adequate junior college system to take up the burden. By 1916, however, Stanford felt the pressure of the dynamic growth of the University of California. With a self-image as a relatively small, privately endowed university unable to compete with large, tax-supported state institutions in size of student body, faculty, and physical plant, Stanford adopted a numerical limitation for all undergraduates matriculating into the lower division. More stringent entrance requirements began to plague male as well as female applicants for admission.

As the number of applicants grew and entrance became somewhat more competitive for male students, alumni opposition to the stricter entrance requirements grew sharply by the end of the decade. Led primarily by those who supported fraternities and athletics, the opposition equated "limitation" with "elimination" of the undergraduate curriculum and therefore of "college life" from the Stanford campus. The drop in applications and enrollment during the Depression, however, soon would deflate the issue.

The student body was not the only campus group to feel the tightening of the reins. In many ways the faculty, too, benefited from the attentiveness of the administration with improved salaries, benefits, loans, research funds, and facilities. They paid with the loss of their influence on the individual student and a lessening role in student extracurricular affairs generally, but found a new voice in a more organized Academic Council and a more effective committee structure.

Stanford's first professional school—Medicine—established a precedent for the linking of like departments with similar academic, budgetary, and physical needs. The university moved in a slow but carefully choreographed effort to gather the many independent and virtually autonomous departments under school umbrellas: Education (1917), Biological Sciences (1922), Nursing (1922), Social Sciences (1923), Law (1923), Engineering (1924), Physical Sciences (1925), Letters (1925). And a new Graduate School of Business was added in 1924. Although the number and configuration would change several times over the next 30 years, the hierarchy of university-school-department would remain intact.

As the prosperous 1920's unfolded, Stanford was at a crisis in its development. Its ambitions had grown quickly, but inflation took its toll on the university endowment. Wilbur's ambitious wish list—to improve faculty salaries and benefits, to build new dormitories and teaching and research facilities, to improve the Medical School, scholarships, and the water supply, and to expand library and scientific collections—pointed to the need to find financial support beyond the conservatively invested endowment, to gain alumni and public support, and to "depersonalize" the family trust so closely associated with the wealthy founders.

The university slowly changed its highly conservative approach to fund-raising as well as investment in order to improve the Stanford endowment. In a series of campaigns for one, two, then three million dollars, the university set in motion major efforts at attracting outside support. Land use was reviewed, beginning with the sale of the Stanford family's farmlands at Vina and Gridley. Land-use experiments were explored. Some were short-lived: a possible game refuge, a proposed hotel, a school of aviation. Others directly benefited the community at home, such as new leasing arrangements for faculty housing.

For the first time, outside funding played an active role in the development of the academic and research program. By the time the Ryan High Voltage Laboratory was opened on Stanford Avenue in 1926, much of Professor Harris J. Ryan's research agenda was well underway, but the Ryan Lab was an impressive operation funded by the City of Los Angeles and five electrical power companies interested in the development of high-voltage power lines. A year later, money from the Daniel Guggenheim Fund for the Promotion of Aeronautics made possible the remodeling of a building for the research of professors William Durand and E. P. Lesley on propeller design.

Many people made their mark on the Stanford that emerged from World War I. Among its deans and president, its faculty and football coaches, its student body presidents and alumni leaders, few had as sweeping an impact in the mind of the community as alumnus and Board of Trustees member Herbert Hoover. His attentions had remained steady since his graduation in 1895, and his benefactions had begun as quiet but well-placed gifts for scholarships, book collections, and building construction. The benefits of his reorganization of the university's financial management were largely hidden to the Stanford student, but his orchestration of community support for a Stanford "Union," aimed at promoting informal social contact among students, faculty, and alumni, provided a much-appreciated center for student activities.

The benefactions mounted. The Hoover War Collection, begun in 1919 in the main library, would grow dramatically over the decade. In 1921, the Food Research Institute, created from Carnegie Foundation funding prompted by Hoover, began its studies of Soviet agriculture and world wheat economy. The new Graduate School of Business, the second after Harvard's to be established in the country, opened in 1926 with funding marshalled by Hoover, at that time Secretary of Commerce.

The self-confident and energized Stanford community, thus, was not surprised as Hoover proceeded with such dynamism and success, not only as an engineer, but as director of the Commission for Relief in Belgium and later as head of the U.S. Food Administration during the war, as Secretary of Commerce under President Coolidge, and in 1928 as the Republican candidate for president. Breaking with its avowed nonpartisan tradition, Stanford erupted with enthusiasm. The *Stanford Illustrated Review* devoted an entire issue to Hoover's campaign and the 1928 *Quad* was dedicated to him. Never before, or since, had the Alumni Association endorsed a presidential candidate, but in 1928 its board formally spoke out for Hoover. Even the faculty put partisan debate aside and united to telegraph Hoover their congratulations at his nomination and their appreciation of the honor this reflected on his young alma mater.

At home at Stanford before beginning the presidential campaign, Hoover broke political custom at Wilbur's suggestion. Rather than accept his party's nomination in a small, private ceremony at home weeks after the convention, he delivered his acceptance speech to a crowd of over 70,000 in Stanford Stadium and to millions by radio broadcast.

Months later, Hoover returned to Stanford to cast his vote at the polling station at the Women's Clubhouse of the Stanford Union. At word of his victory later that night, a large crowd assembled before the Hoover house on San Juan Hill, joined by news cameras and radio hookups. Across the country radio listeners heard the celebration—the Souza marches, the "Star-Spangled Banner," and, in closing, some 2,000 students singing "Hail, Stanford, Hail."

Herbert Hoover took to the White House firmly held values he associated with his Stanford education—self-reliance, hard work, and a commitment to Leland Stanford's vision of "direct usefulness in life." And with him, as Secretary of the Interior and closest cabinet confidant, would go Stanford University's own president, Ray Lyman Wilbur.

The quintessential Stanford man at his desk: Ray Lyman Wilbur, '96, during his student days in Encina and later in the president's office.

Medical school dean Wilbur, waiting with Chancellor Jordan before his inauguration as Stanford's third president.

*Community support for
Belgian relief during World War I
took on town-gown dimen-
sions at the popular European
Market on the Circle in
Palo Alto, 1914 and 1915.*

Chancellor Jordan receives a boutonniere; May Hopkins (left), wife of Board of Trustees president Timothy Hopkins, strolls with Lou Henry Hoover.

Stanford women joined the war effort, including Professor Clelia Mosher in American Red Cross uniform in France, 1917.

Stanford's second ambulance corps left San Francisco for France in November 1916 with this sign on its train window.

Jordan's reputedly pacifist campus changed markedly as the United States entered the European war. The Student Army Training Corps shows off its drill in the Inner Quad.

After a year in France, the ambulance corps served on the Balkan front, with headquarters in Koritza, Albania.

Stanford Mother's Club tea on the Women's Clubhouse balcony in 1929: completed in 1916, the clubhouse was a popular center for faculty women, alumnae, and undergraduates. It would later be joined by a men's clubhouse and a union building.

The arcades of the Inner Quad are timeless, but buildings are going up all around: Thomas Welton Stanford, Leland Stanford's youngest brother, donated both his Australian art collection and the Art Gallery (above) to house it; the new President's House sits on the knoll, 1919.

The new Roble Hall was completed in 1918; old Roble, transformed into a men's dorm, was then renamed Sequoia Hall.

With two-thirds of the student body living in fraternities and sororities, the university decided to build more dormitories, including baronial Toyon, to redirect student attention toward more "democratic" housing.

As collegiate life entered popular American culture, Hollywood discovered Stanford: a 1924 publicity shot for "Stanford Days" featured Hal Bumbaugh, '24, and Peggy Richardson, '22. Lloyd Nolan, '26, also appeared in the film.

*Students made it to Port-
land in 27 hours driving
this 1920 model-T touring
car in 1927. It took Lind-
bergh the same time to cross
the Atlantic that year, they
noted. Headed to a Pacific
Conference Advertising
Club speaking contest were
(left to right) Ted Baer, '27,
Samuel Cochrane, '29,
Louis Creveling, '28, and
Robert Hume, '29.*

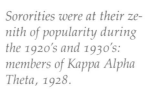

Quiet on the Row: Kappa Kappa Gamma and the elms of Lasuen.

Sororities were at their zenith of popularity during the 1920's and 1930's: members of Kappa Alpha Theta, 1928.

Women of Alpha Omicron Pi "stage an aviation party as newest campus social stunt" in front of their chapter house, reported the "Stanford Illustrated Review" in 1919.

Hester Proctor's scrapbook records her Gamma Phi Beta sisters of 1918–22, but—the usual fate of the photographer—not herself.

Stanford's 24 fraternities vied with "Hall men" for control of student politics and publications. Beta Theta Pi albums document several decades of fraternity men and life in the Beta house.

Breakers Club.
1921-22.

Frank Chuck, '22, Ph.D. '25 in chemistry (fourth from left standing in group, and in cap and gown) was among those who inaugurated the Chinese Student Association's clubhouse on Salvatierra Street. Residents renovated an older home with financial help from local Chinese businessmen.

Eating clubs provided fraternal camaraderie for Hall men at less than half the price. The highly popular Breakers, posing for their "Quad" portrait in 1921, included track, football, and baseball men in 1921–22. Dink Templeton (fifth from left, back row), who studied for his law degree while coaching the Stanford track team, is identified by a club mate as "Boy Coach."

At Stanford, class presidents were just as frequently hashers as they were golfers: two hashers serving up the fare at the Los Arcos eating club, 1929.

Lagunita and a crowded boathouse are the setting for jousting canoeists at the annual Water Carnival.

Cars are not simply a campus status symbol but also central to many a Stanford prank: members of Toyon Club, including a 1926 ASSU president, pose before (left) and after (right); roadsters on the steps of Sequoia.

With the ratio of men to women reaching 5 to 1, spring festivities are bound to include a comment on the Stanford "500" from both men and women.

As part of Junior Week, the "Irish Marathon" pitted teams from each class and an additional group of "holdovers" in a race around campus. The holdovers, costumed in typical Stanford fashion, conducted the race in less than serious fashion.

The Frosh-Soph Tie-Up, as strong a tradition as ever, was "softened" a bit by the addition of water—turning it into the annual Frosh-Soph Mudfight.

Students march to the new stadium, site of the upcoming Tie-Up battle. Each side tries to tie up as many opponents as possible as spectators cheer. Use of knives, cleated shoes, and slugging was banned by 1930.

On Rough's Day, Stanford men caricature the less refined, but still not vanished, days of the pioneer classes. It's yet another chance to give everyone— especially freshmen and coeds—a ribbing.

Mule teams move dirt for the new Stanford stadium, cutting the playing field to 23 feet below ground level and building up the sides for seating.

Completed in 1921, the stadium was enlarged twice during the 1920's until it could seat more than 89,000.

President Wilbur, interested in Stanford sports from his student days, kicks off at the first rugby game played on the new field.

All-time All-American Ernie Nevers, '26, as Cardinal fullback.

Nevers (second from left) and coach Glenn "Pop" Warner (with cigar) put Stanford on the national football map in the mid-1920's.

American football returned to Stanford after the war and with it a more amiable athletic agreement with the University of California: Stanford scores in the 1928 Big Game.

The Big Game bonfire, bigger than ever in 1921.

The 1928 varsity team, on its trip east to play West Point in New York, exercises while the train stops in North Platte, Nebraska. Stanford beat the favored cadets 26-0.

Precision in card stunts was the mark of the Stanford rooting section, as seen at Big Game, 1924.

Stanford songleaders before the era of the "Dollies."

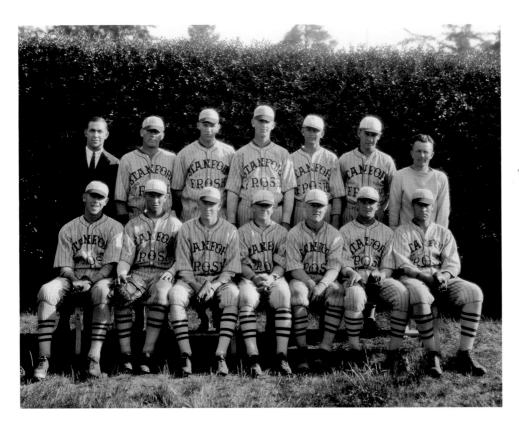

A freshmen baseball team poses with all-around coach Ernest P. "Husky" Hunt.

Outspoken Richard "Dink" Templeton, standing with "Dad" Moulton, was 24 when he began his coaching career at Stanford (1921–39). His teams won three national collegiate titles, and his hard-driving charges set sixteen world records and won nine Olympic medals.

USC's Charley Paddock uses his famous flying finish to beat Stanford's Morris Kirksey, '22, in the 100-yard dash. Kirksey won a gold medal in the 1920 Olympics in the 400-meter relay and set a world record in the 100 meters a year later.

George Green, '27, sliding during Stanford–Santa Clara game of 1921.

A double gold medalist at the 1920 Olympics, Norman Ross, '20, returns to the Encina pool for an exhibition race.

Ernie Brandsten with two of his many top divers—1928 gold medal winner Pete Des Jardins, '32, and 1924 silver medalist Dave Fall, '27. Brandsten coached Stanford swimmers for more than 31 years and was U.S. diving coach in four Olympic games.

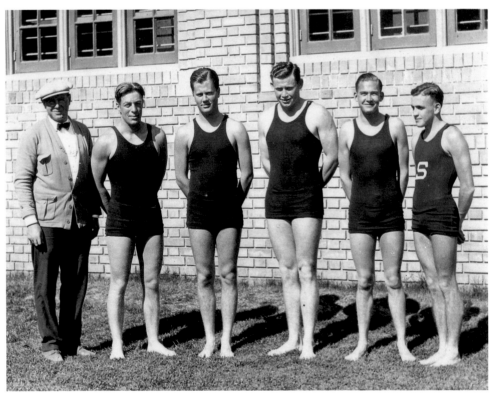

The 1926 Cardinal swim team poses next to the Encina pool.

Track women are still in bloomers in the 1920's, but an active Women's Athletic Association fields intercollegiate hockey and basketball teams as well as interclass teams in archery, swimming, tennis, and track.

Photo from one of Palo Alto photographer Berton Crandall's proof albums. Students most likely knew the identity of this unlabeled drawing room farce of 1917.

"Oedipus Rex," produced on the Museum steps on a warm August night in 1924, was jointly directed by Gordon Davis of Stanford and Evalyn Thomas of the University of California, Southern Branch (soon to be UCLA).

The Stanford Museum of Art, by daylight.

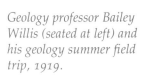

Geology professor Bailey Willis (seated at left) and his geology summer field trip, 1919.

David Starr Jordan (top center) relaxes with faculty and friends.

Highly influential Mary Yost, Dean of Women, played a major role in the lives of Stanford women— sorority and hall. During a hike, she sits with faculty friends Frances T. Russell (left) and Elisabeth Buckingham (center) of the English Department.

Psychology and education professor Lewis M. Terman pioneered in research on gifted children and intelligence.

A silver teapot adorns a faculty picnic on the beach south of Carmel in 1922; seated at center is historian Edgar E. Robinson.

The Ryan High Voltage Laboratory on Stanford Avenue, the first Stanford research lab to be supported by extensive outside funding, perfected transmission of high-voltage power over long distances.

Harris J. Ryan and his wife enjoy an outing in 1905, the year they arrived at Stanford.

Engineering professor William F. Durand, a leader in the study of propeller design, directed research at the new Guggenheim Aeronautic Laboratory located in the engineering lab buildings.

The Stanford University
Medical School and clinics
remained in San Francisco
until 1959. The buildings
stood at the corner of
Webster and Sacramento
streets.

Local mothers and children
learn more about nutrition
at the Children's Clinic of
the Medical School.

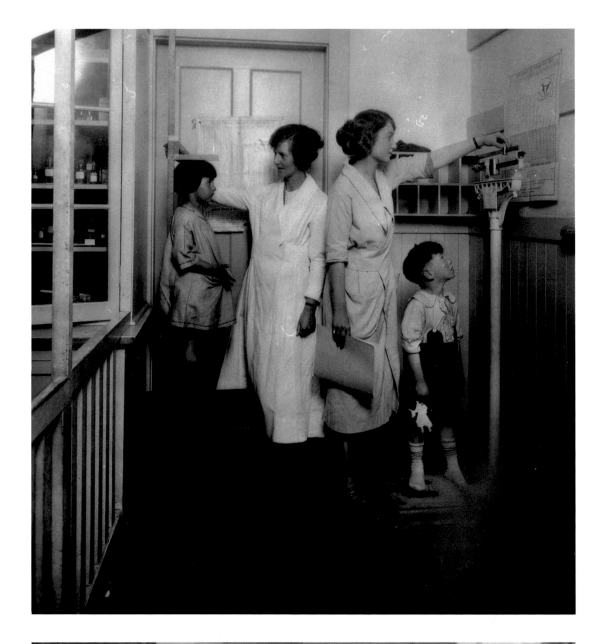

Weighing in at the Children's Clinic.

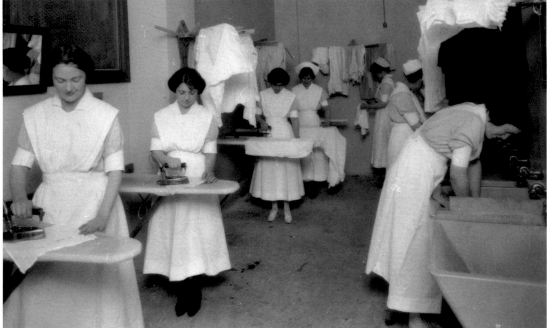

Laundry at the new building of Stanford's School of Nursing, San Francisco, 1922.

Herbert Hoover, of Stanford's Pioneer Class of '95, brought major organizational changes and a spurt of university growth during his service as a member of the Board of Trustees.

Hoover accepted the Republican Party nomination for president of the United States in a speech before a standing-room-only crowd at Stanford stadium. Here Hoover enters the stadium with his wife, Lou, and son Allan (standing), a Stanford undergraduate.

At the Hoover House on San Juan Hill, the Stanford community celebrates the presidential election of their favorite son in November 1928. John Philip Sousa, on campus to direct a concert, leads the band in marches and "Hail, Stanford, Hail" as hundreds of thousands across the country listen by radio.

214

Searsville Lake in the Stanford foothills, destination of many a campus hiker and university field trip since the 1890's, is now part of the Jasper Ridge Biological Preserve.

The Depression Era, 1929-1940

Students of today may seem scornful of those things which have sentimental value to us. What they are doing is seeking release from custom-made habit. They want the same freedom to express themselves that gave ruggedness to pioneer Stanford.

CAROL GREEN WILSON, '14, 1934

In October 1929, the distant Wall Street stock market crash received little comment in the *Stanford Daily*. More news space was devoted to what was viewed by many as a truly depressing event—the passing of the Toonerville Trolley on October 20. A campus institution since 1909, the Peninsula Railway's red trolley line had been the community's first step away from buggy and bicycle transportation. But two decades later cars abounded on campus and in the neighborhood. With ridership and profits declining, the trolley was replaced by a motor bus.

The year 1929 opened brightly for Stanford, with respected alumni serving as president and as first lady of the United States. University president Ray Lyman Wilbur took a leave of absence to join the Hoover cabinet as Secretary of the Interior. Classics professor Augustus Taber Murray moved to Washington at Herbert Hoover's request to head the Society of Friends congregation attended by the president's family, and many alumni took administrative posts. Much to the amusement of students, flocks of out-of-state visitors roamed the campus in search of the Hoover residence as the Stanford community enjoyed the glories, and suffered the scrutiny, accorded each presidential hometown.

Stanford athletics also had brought much public attention to campus. Glenn "Pop" Warner's football teams, reflecting Warner's love of surprises and powerful play, captured the imagination of the public. Stanford Olympians had done well in the 1928 Amsterdam games, winning four gold medals—Pete Des Jardins's two in diving, Bud Spencer's as a member of the 1600-meter relay team, and Bill King's in the high jump.

The Farm glowed with prosperity and confidence. In the spring of 1929, most of the old sheds and barns of the stock farm were removed to make way for the new 18-hole 185-acre golf course. Nearby, a modern concrete bridge crossing San Francisquito Creek replaced the old wooden bridge that had recently collapsed under the weight of a large tourist bus. Campus residents heartily welcomed improvements at Felt Lake that helped meet the demands for water from increasing residential and landscaping use. And a new gymnasium for women, the second Roble Gym, had

just been completed near the women's dormitory, providing a large gym room, dance studio, game room, and sun porches.

Although the panic of the stock market crash at first seemed distant and curious to Stanford students, the West soon would be caught up in the economic trauma of the Depression. By 1930, breadlines were forming in San Francisco. To the south, family farms and orchards, once the lifeblood of the "Valley of Heart's Delight," suffocated under overdue bills and unpaid mortgages and fell to a new kind of neighbor, the corporate owner. In Palo Alto, the homeless camped along San Francisquito Creek until a shelter was established in 1931.

While some graduating seniors of 1929 and 1930 had to struggle to find jobs, it was later classes, especially those graduating after 1931, which were surprised to discover that the world no longer had a sure spot for college graduates. The Depression also caught up with enrolled students and their parents, who faced rising costs of tuition, room, and board with shrinking incomes and savings. With extensive financial aid a thing of the future, many students looked for part-time work, competing with schoolmates and the local unemployed for a decreasing number of jobs. Even local farms and orchards, once a sure source for seasonal income during summer and fall harvesting, hired fewer students as owners turned to migrant workers at lower wages.

Yet the nationwide economic depression did not spell a return to the Stanford of the pioneer years, with its camaraderie of struggle and commitment to the working student. Instead, the Depression accentuated changes underway while promoting new ones. Composition of the student body narrowed to a more homogeneous group from middle and upper socioeconomic backgrounds, largely Anglo-Saxon, Protestant, and conservative, and Stanford acquired a new and remarkably different public image, abetted by idyllic climate and pastoral spaciousness: the country club of California universities.

Tuition inevitably narrowed the student body's diversity. It also prompted a dramatic change in gender ratio on campus. Instituted in 1920 to help support an ambitious program of growth, tuition became crucial to maintaining status quo by the early 1930's. But because of the Depression, the university faced dwindling male enrollments for the first time in its history—down by more than 15 percent in just three years—and the subsequent loss of tuition money. The motive of the Board of Trustees in lifting the quota of 500 female registrants was unashamedly financial.

The ratio of women to men had been dropping steadily, and by 1933, it was less than one woman to six men. Academic requirements for women applicants were significantly more stringent than for men. Those unaware of the original commitment to coeducation often assumed that Stanford had been established as a men's school.

The artificial social condition provoked by the limitation had been a topic of student discussion for years, with student commentators arguing for more normal and balanced contact with the opposite sex and against the "lopsided education, double standard, and discrimination against the women of the 500." In the 1930 Women's Edition of the *Daily*, Sylvia Weaver, women's editor, wrote: "There is the traditional attitude toward Stanford women. Mills girls are beautiful,

California's coeds are good dates . . . but Stanford women have high I.Q.'s. There is a deep rooted ancient prejudice against the Five Hundred, and although there are always exceptions—that doesn't help the rule. Not a whit." The *Daily* was also filled with comments on the lighter side of the limitation: "The trite saying 'Four out of five have "It," the fifth goes to Stanford' is counteracted by the opinion of one popular coed: 'Four out of five men are conceited. All four go to Stanford.'"[1]

The limitation also tied the hands of the university during the financial crisis of the early 1930's. Since there had long been many more applications from women than could be admitted, the route to gaining more tuition-paying students without dropping academic standards was obvious. On May 11, 1933, the Board of Trustees announced a Santa Clara County Superior Court ruling allowing it to overturn the limit imposed by Mrs. Stanford's 1899 amendment to the Founding Grant. The Board concluded that the number of women should be substantially the same proportion of total enrollment as existed when Mrs. Stanford set the original 500 limit, or around 45 percent.

The next day's *Daily* headline read "Brash move is taken to bolster fiscal condition." At Roble Hall, there was "a gasp of astonishment, followed by a long hearty booing" from women whose minority status had given them a distinct social advantage amid the sea of male faces on campus.[2]

Some 800 women enrolled that next fall, and by the decade's end, female enrollment had more than tripled the original allotment to 1,722. The demographic change placed enormous pressure on available student housing. By fall 1933, two floors of the Stanford Union had been remodeled and three houses on Salvatierra—Mariposa House, Madrono, and Elm Cot-

tage—reassigned as women's residences. Faculty homes as well as Castilleja School and Miss Harker's Academy in Palo Alto also made room until Lagunita Court could be completed later in 1934. And beginning that year, all freshmen women were assigned to one dormitory, Roble Hall, just as all freshmen men lived at Encina.

But even with the new dormitory, Stanford's nine sororities—unchanged since the days of the 500—attempted to house a large proportion of the female students each year, and competition for admission to one of the nine grew fierce and ever more controversial. Concern over the growing social and political divergence between "sorority women" and "hall women," complicated by complaints of parents over the distractions—or disappointments—of sorority rushing, loomed over the office of the Dean of Women. The stage was set for a dramatic review of the sorority system in the early 1940's.

At the opposite side of campus, Stanford men not living in the 24 fraternities resided at Encina, Toyon, Sequoia, and Branner halls. Most were members of the seven eating clubs that had been established during the previous three decades, housed in new quarters behind Encina Hall in "Encina Commons" and near Toyon. Visitors from other campuses were impressed with the strong identity of the hall and eating club men, who were an important factor in student activities, particularly key areas of student politics and publications. Meanwhile, the Interfraternity Council continued to deal with problems of financial, scholastic, and social responsibility. Yet throughout the 1930's many a chapter house along "the Row"—fraternity and sorority—received a face-lift or was rebuilt completely with the help of alumni.

The campus community was proud of its relative calm during the Depression, years that saw turbulence, even rioting, at other campuses. Stanford maintained its reputation as a progressive institution despite its conservative leadership and conservative student body, in part because the administration chose to treat bursts of student activism with notable restraint. Despite his enormous influence over student affairs, Wilbur rarely interfered with selection of speakers or topics in student publications. On a number of occasions, he overruled the more conservative executive board of the ASSU to permit wider freedom of expression through student publications or events.

The number of college activists at Stanford was, in fact, quite small. Although a socialist Norman-Thomas-for-President Club was established in 1932 and other small student political organizations came and went through the decade, and students like *Daily* editor Abe Mellinkoff reminded the community of the grim reality beyond campus boundaries, student interest more typically was excited by football than by a controversial speaker. In straw polls in elections throughout the 1920's and 1930's, students voted Republican by at least a 2-to-1 margin, including a more than 3-to-1 margin for Hoover over Roosevelt in 1932. Those students active in political or social protest seldom challenged the university administration's right to make decisions regarding their activities and concentrated on promoting economic change from within the established system.

As the number of students had increased over the decades, social regulations grew not only in number but in complexity, carefully monitored by student government and the administration. Regulations originally aimed at protecting Stanford women from the aggressions of soldiers stationed at nearby Camp Fremont—the 10:30 P.M. curfew for women or restric-

tions on couples walking in the hills without a chaperone, for example—never had been lifted as promised. Nor, for the most part, did the women object. Although they had played no role in the formulation of the regulations, the women took on their enforcement in June 1930 through the Women's Council and Women's Conference of the Associated Women Students. It would be left to the student activists of the 1960's to challenge the *in loco parentis* legacy of the Wilbur years.

Academic matters also became more complex. Undergraduates were far more familiar with their deans of women and men than with the academic dean of their chosen school. And an idiosyncratic system of points computed a student's standing, showing the grade point level in relation to units completed. These comparative numbers were published for all to see in the *Stanford Register*, the quarterly directory, affectionately nicknamed the "Bawl Out."

In 1934, the Academic Council decided that it would not flunk out students unable to maintain scholarship but would rely on the common sense of the failing student to know when it was time to withdraw from the university. Critics dubbed it the "No-fault" system, suggesting that tuition was more important than scholarship. But the Academic Council echoed its predecessors' trust that students would either make their way or leave of their own accord.

By 1932, the depths of the Depression, tuition put a crimp in the spending money of just about everyone. But social life hardly abated; it simply was relocated closer to campus and, in fact, increased in offerings. Although the trip up to the City on the new four-lane Bayshore Highway made more convenient the "big dates" of dancing at the "St. Frantic" (the St. Francis Hotel) or the "Mark" (the Mark Hopkins), campus dances and social events on the Row often took their place. A new series of "Depression Dances" began on campus in 1931, costing only ten cents admission. But equally popular were dances like the Toyon Formal, at $3.50 per couple, which, according to the *Daily*, included: "Neon signs, black and gold decorations, Gordon Heche's ten-piece orchestra and a limited number of bids."[3]

Women in particular found new freedom in more local entertainments. In an interview of Stanford student leaders in 1933 on their impressions of how the Depression had affected campus life, Marion Slonaker, Kappa Alpha Theta president, commented: "Before, we used to think we couldn't go to a show unless a boyfriend took us. Now a bunch of us girls go together, sit in the cheapest seats, and find out we have just as much fun without any men—and sometimes better."[4]

Dean Mary Yost feared that the increasingly active social program detracted from the normally high scholarship record of women students. In her report to the president in 1935, she expressed concern that there was "a growing tendency on the part of some students to regard the University as a country club rather than as an educational institution." While the women's standing collectively was, as usual, notably above that of the men, it was lower than the year before, which in turn had been lower than the previous year—the final year of the elite 500.

The "country club" image to which Dean Yost referred had become a very sensitive issue. In a 1931 story about Stanford and the controversy surrounding discussion of eliminating the lower-division curriculum, *Time* magazine recounted the impressive accomplishments of Stanford's scholar-president David Starr Jordan, but went on to an exaggerated description of contemporary Stanford as "predominantly a rich man's college" with "one of the finest Pacific Coast golf courses, two lakes, a polo field as well as two great gymnasiums and many a smaller playing field and game court" in addition to its 90,000-seat football stadium. "Though it is their custom to affect corduroy trousers, lumberjack shirts and other unassuming gear," the article continued, "more than half [the men] own automobiles. Some fly their own planes."[5]

Fueling the country club image were two surveys conducted in the mid-1930's which ranked Stanford lower than expected academically and significantly lower than the University of California. In the 1935 national survey published in the *Atlantic Monthly*, Edward R. Embree rated Cal fourth in the country in academic prowess and Stanford twelfth, with the statement, "When we are considering scholarly eminence of universities, the country club aspects of undergraduate life are not relevant."[6]

Alumni joined students in expressing their concern and surprise at this new image, one that they viewed as unfair and one that would take decades to live down. But the Depression era was a turning point in Stanford's self-image as well as public image. Early in the decade, the ASSU handbook carefully listed traditions, many going back 40 years: no smoking on the Quad, no pool playing on Sundays, corduroys worn only by upperclassman, the Honor System. But little was said of the many traditions that had fallen by the wayside.[7]

By 1930, the Plug Ugly battles between the juniors and seniors were long gone, as were the Baseball Fights between freshmen and sophomores, Poster Fights and Washington's Day Parades, Rough's Day and Encina Hall raids, tubbing, and the worst of hazing. The Tie-up now was closely regulated, with knives, cleated shoes, and slugging banned by ASSU bylaws.

The legendary Stanford Rough had all but disappeared. Almost as much a part of Stanford legend as Leland, Jane, and Leland Jr., the Rough was mourned in a special 1931 issue of the *Chaparral*. "He feared not man nor beast," eulogized Chappie's equally mythical "Old Boy": "Beer was the standard beverage, and cords the standard pants. Sweaters served as shirts,

and Roughs served at table. Stanford was the Farm, and anybody who got fancy just wasn't the sort of guy they wanted around."[8]

"Old Boy" admitted that his was an outdated, sentimentalized picture, but he suggested that the Rough had represented "something carefree and natural that was Stanford," something of the spirit that had encouraged poor men from the Camp to be campus editors and working students from Encina to become campus political leaders. If the Rough once had challenged the notion that a university education was only for the sons of the affluent, now students and alumni were intrigued with Stanford's latest nickname, "the Harvard of the West." Mourning the Rough on the one hand, the *Chaparral* also carried a series of Chevrolet advertisements throughout 1931 enticing the Stanford audience with scenes of fellow collegians at Harvard, Notre Dame, and Princeton. Similarly, four dapper young Stanford men posed at the Stanford Golf Course with the latest Ford Deluxe Phaeton convertible.

The vacuum of lost custom quickly filled with enthusiasm for collegiate sports and the traditions surrounding them. Stanford of the 1930's had an impressive football legacy from the 1920's and "Pop" Warner's teams. The win-at-all-costs style of collegiate football continued to plague university faculty and administrations across the country, but Warner's successor, coach Tiny Thornhill, had a different approach to the game. To Thornhill, the game belonged to the boys and should remain a game; the players on his teams were at Stanford primarily to get an education. The lack of harsh discipline, of curfews, and of long strategy sessions were a curiosity, and the players, dubbed "laughing boys," were criticized for not taking the game seriously. But if their practice field antics seemed peculiar, their success became legendary. In 1932, as freshmen, they suffered an embarrassing loss to the University of Southern California and vowed never to lose to USC again. The next year, in their first varsity season, the "Vow Boys" redeemed their pledge with a 13–7 victory over the Trojans. The Vow Boys never lost to USC, or to Cal, and earned a 25-4-2 record and three trips to the Rose Bowl, 1933–35.

Stanford's 1939 team, which won only a single game, however, was characterized by a former Vow Boy as "the worst group of players who have ever worn the Stanford red." But in colorful new uniforms and introducing a revitalized T-formation, Clark Shaughnessy's 1940 team emulated the Vow Boys. Much to everyone's surprise and pleasure, the "Wow Boys" were undefeated in regular season play and, on New Year's Day, won a Rose Bowl victory.

Stanford rose to basketball stardom in the second half of the decade with another team of "laughing boys." Led by team captain Hank Luisetti, Cardinal teams won Pacific Coast Conference titles three years in a row. In 1936, Stanford met Long Island University in Madison Square Garden. Eastern sports writers were stunned to watch Long Island's 43-game winning streak ended as Stanford players passed, ran, laughed, and pushed up the score, and Luisetti displayed his innovative running one-handed jump shot. In an era that rarely saw college teams score more than 50 points a game, Luisetti would set an individual record by scoring 50 points in one game as he led Stanford to a 92–27 romp over Duquesne on New Year's Eve, 1937. His one-handed shooting would change basketball forever.

Meanwhile, women's sports finally moved out of black bunting and bloomers into tennis shorts and sailing pants, duly recorded in fashion-plate photographs in the *Quad*. Women signed up for archery, basketball, hockey, swimming, tennis, and hiking, and the women's Block "S" letter was awarded to those passing high standards of sportsmanship, scholarship, and posture. While the posture requirement may have harkened back to earlier days, the health code of the Women's Athletic Association also reflected more modern times; along with recommendations on adequate sleep and cold showers was the admonition "no excessive smoking."

The beginning of the decade also saw the return of an old tradition and the acquisition of a new one: in 1930, Stanford would steal back the Axe and pick up a mascot.

Despite the rivalries with USC and UCLA, to Stanford's student body the real "enemy" remained the University of California at Berkeley, and the symbol of that enmity was the Stanford Axe. Since 1899, the California student body had taunted Stanford rooting sections with the stolen axe, returning it to a Berkeley bank vault in an armored car after each game or rally. Cal cheerleaders even had appropriated the "Give 'em the axe" yell of Stanford's pioneer classes. Attempts to recapture the Axe were unsuccessful until April 3, 1930.

In an elaborate ruse concocted by the "Immortal 21" of Sequoia Hall, a "press photographer" set off a double dose of flash powder, blinding Cal's Axe chaperones as the Axe was on its way back to its vault. One of the Immortals grabbed the Axe and threw it into the waiting getaway car, while another tossed tear gas into the confused crowd. As the car made its escape, other Immortals, planted in the crowd, added

to the confusion by encouraging the Cal contingent to regroup by the Campanile. Somehow all 21 made their way safely back to Palo Alto. The campus was in an uproar when the Axe arrived at the Quad at 7:50 P.M.

The next day, the *Stanford Daily* shouted "Axe Regained" in a 5-inch-high banner headline, while the *Daily Californian* moaned "Axe Stolen." The clash made front-page headlines statewide. Classes were canceled, and the university presented each of the "Immortal 21" with a Block "S" and a special gold Axe watch charm. Reported the editor of the *Quad* later that year, "This event ranks in importance with Xenophon's march, Hannibal's crossing of the Alps, and anybody's flight to the moon."[9]

The contraband once again was placed in a bank vault, this time in Palo Alto. While the two university administrations fretted over the potential violence of retribution, the two student body governments haggled over a solution. Finally, in 1933, the associated students of both universities agreed that the Axe would be awarded yearly to the winner of the Big Game.

Since the first Big Game in spring 1892, Stanford had been identified with its dramatic cardinal red color. School colors long had distinguished sides on the playing field, instilled pride, and promoted campus identity. With the upsurge of popular interest in collegiate sports during the 1920's, the idea of a mascot took hold—personified on the field, adorning uniforms, and chasing each other across sports pages. The University of California used the state symbol of the grizzly. Washington had its cougar, Southern California the Trojan. Even the newly established second campus of the University of California near Los Angeles had taken the California derivative of "bruin." Stanford, too, would officially adopt a mascot.

The Stanford Indian had first appeared in 1923, the idea of Dr. Tom Williams, class of '97, a former varsity football player, an original member of the Board of Athletic Control, and an avid supporter of Stanford sports. The idea was not entirely original—college and high school teams across the country had been adopting variations on the American Indian theme. At Stanford, supporters stirred interest in newly excavated burial mounds found on campus and portrayed the symbol as lord and conquerer of the various animals chosen by Stanford's Pacific Conference opponents. In addition, they pointed to endless possibilities for pageantry and costume at rallies and games, with exuberant use of cardinal red. "Pop" Warner's teams, dressed in red pants, were dubbed "redskins," then "Indians," in part recalling Warner's earlier association with the Carlisle Indian School.

Although the students soon lost interest, alumni and the news media kept alive the informal association between the university and the Indian mascot throughout the 1920's. With the Axe back in Palo Alto in 1930, that fall's Big Game promised to be a classic battle. Official or not, Indians were chasing bears, and bears Indians, in headlines, editorials, and cartoons in newspaper sports sections throughout the West. After an emotional rally laden with Indian symbolism, the ASSU Executive Committee unanimously adopted the Indian as Stanford's symbol. The motif appeared everywhere—student publications, athletic jackets, university stationery, and advertisements in campus publications. Cardinal red continued to symbolize Stanford as well, and "the Cardinal" would be used interchangeably with the Indian both on and off campus.

In the fall of 1937, the Stanford Indian became identified for the first time with the cartoon character "Li'l Injun" created by Tommy Thompson for the *Stanford Daily*. This "shirtless, wide-eyed, boyish" figure would be further caricatured during the 1940's by Bob Breer. With his big nose, bald head, and dangling single feather, Li'l Injun became as much a part of Stanford symbolism as the highly romanticized, Hiawatha-like figure of the Indian warrior. In 1972, however, the student body voted to discontinue the mascot on the grounds it represented an offensive ethnic stereotype. Unable to agree on a new mascot, the student body and Athletic Department returned to the sole use of Stanford's singular, vibrant cardinal red.

From 1916 to World War II, the Stanford athletic program owed much of its success to the management of the Board of Athletic Control (BAC). The Board, in turn, relied on the business acumen, creativity, kindness, and loyalty of Emmanuel B. "Sam" McDonald. First employed at Stanford in 1903 to work on the foundations of new wings to the Museum, McDonald worked his way up to serve as superintendent of athletic buildings and grounds, the first black employee in Stanford history to attain a supervisory position. During the financially troubled times of World War I and later during the Depression, McDonald always found a way to take care of the athletes' needs, at times at his own expense.

McDonald had much to do with maintaining the ambience, as well as the friendliness, of the Farm. His small herd of sheep served as "Sam's animated lawn mowers" for years, and the garden behind his home, the brick Track House, was renowned for its vegetables. But more important were his skill and business sense, which created a new source of income for the athletic program. McDonald persuaded the BAC to lease land from the university for agricultural income purposes. Located primarily around the arboretum, various parcels of land felt McDonald's magic touch and within a few years not only produced enough hay to feed the sheep but also to turn a profit in hay, sheep, and cattle.

Beyond his contributions to the management of the athletic facilities and their support, Sam McDonald held as influential a place in student hearts as had the charismatic Jordan. In 1939, he was honored with the naming of Sam McDonald Road (now Mall) between Angell Field and today's Tennis Stadium. Through the years, he wisely invested his modest earnings, acquiring land near La Honda in the mountains behind the campus. Before his death in 1957, he had donated his

450 acres for public use. The area is now enjoyed as Sam McDonald Park.

McDonald was also associated with one of the most long-standing traditions of the years between the two world wars—Con Home Day. The Stanford Home for Convalescent Children, or "Con Home," ancestor of today's Lucile Packard Children's Hospital at Stanford, was founded in May 1920 in what remained of the old Stanford family residence on campus after the earthquake of 1906. The Con Home was operated by a private board that included many prominent Stanford citizens but had no direct relation to, or support from, the university itself. A strained budget made upkeep of the large grounds difficult, and a May "labor day" was proposed. Beginning in the early 1920's Sam McDonald organized the work crew of Stanford's young men and women to paint, wash windows, make repairs, and garden, ending the day with what would become one of its most cherished aspects, the barbecue featuring Chef McDonald and his famous roast lamb, cooked in a deep pit, and baked beans. In 1950, the day was renamed "Sam McDonald Day."

By the 1930's, the Con Home was both an official student charity and benefactor of the university's disciplinary system. It benefited from Con Home work parties, student-run fund-raising drives, solicitations, and entertainments, as well as a demerit system of labor hours at the home for minor disciplinary infractions. Disciplinary action rested with the Men's and Women's Councils, which negotiated with the administration regarding major punishment of suspension or expulsion. But minor offenses—speeding, throwing water balloons down dormitory staircases, raising a ruckus in the library's reading room—caused a quandary. Fines were considered inequitable; five dollars could be much more difficult for one student to pay than for another. The Con Home provided the answer, with fines allotted in number of hours of work assign-

ments—for instance, four hours for waterbagging.

The financial strain of the Depression may not have dampened student spirits, but it continued to be an overwhelming concern to the administration. The university struggled to maintain the level of faculty and staff salaries—and to pay them on time, as it had not been able to do during the economic slump of the 1890's. The university's budget held out until 1933, when the drop in the value of the endowment income forced a salary cut of 10 percent. No faculty members were laid off, and within two years half of that cut would be restored. But it would not be until 1940 that faculty salaries would return to their pre-Depression level.

By 1933, it was clear to the administration that this reputedly rich university was in serious financial trouble. The endowment income, once one of the highest college endowments in the country, had dropped to seventy-fifth, and donations were drying up. Construction had come to a halt, and repairs were kept to a minimum. It was no longer surprising to see a senior faculty member painting his own laboratory walls if he could find, and pay for, the paint himself.

The loss of a major foundation grant for lack of matching gifts and the growing concern at declining alumni support spurred Harry B. Reynolds, member of the class of '96, to gather alumni friends to establish the Stanford Associates, a self-selected group of volunteers who concentrated on soliciting immediate gifts while building a future of gifts through bequests. From this effort grew not only an activist philosophy of university fund raising and an office of development but also a stronger alumni association, a university relations effort, and a professionally staffed news service.

The university encouraged renewed alumni interest in the results of faculty research. Influential teachers and the opportunity to share new ideas with a friendly faculty had made a deep impression on graduates. Young alumni of the class of 1930 came back to campus for a modest lecture series with select faculty arranged by Herbert Wenig, '30. This program was so successful that it was taken up formally three years later by the Alumni Association as an annual day of lectures welcoming graduates back to the Farm. Thus began today's highly successful Alumni Conferences and continuing education programs.

The Depression decade saw little tinkering with the curriculum, although the narrowly defined "Problems of Citizenship" requirement broadened dramatically in 1934 when historian Edgar Eugene Robinson took the lead in the establishment of the "History of Western Civilization" course. Robinson was also responsible for integration of the independent study concept into the undergraduate curriculum. An ancestor of today's department honors programs, independent study encouraged able and ambitious students to work closely with selected faculty on special areas of study. Established in 1925 for upper division students, the program expanded in 1931 and again in 1936 to include exceptional lower division students.

Despite the Depression, Stanford continued to develop from college to true research university, especially in the sciences. Although Stanford was severely limited in its ability to hire new faculty, the Physics Department was able to take advantage of the wave of scientists emigrating from turbulent Europe. Felix Bloch arrived on campus in 1934 knowing little more about Stanford than that it had a department of promising young physicists and that it and a neighboring university stole each other's axes. In the late 1930's, Bloch began his work on nuclear induction, essentially the phenomenon known today as nuclear magnetic resonance, a powerful tool in the analysis of chemical compounds and in diagnostic medicine. In 1952, Bloch became Stanford's first Nobel laureate.

Bloch's colleague William W. Hansen began his collaboration with brothers Russell and Sigurd Varian in 1937, following his first experiments in accelerating electrons. The Physics Department could not pay the Varian brothers as research assistants, but provided free laboratory space and $100 for supplies. Their work with Hansen led to the invention of the klystron microwave tube, a device for generating high-power microwaves that made airborne radar feasible and proved invaluable in Britain's defense during World War II. The klystron would become the cornerstone of California's microelectronics industry and an integral component of high-energy particle accelerators used in medicine and nuclear physics. Within a year following Stanford's licensing of the klystron, the university received its first patent income, strengthening future science and engineering programs.

Trustee Herbert Hoover had predicted that Stanford could be a magnet for business and industrial research and had encouraged academia-industry relations through such efforts as the new Graduate School of Business (1925) and the Food Research Institute (1921). Similarly, Varian Associates, founded in 1949

by the two brothers with colleagues from Stanford's physics department, would stay close to campus. In 1951, at Russell Varian's suggestion, the company was the first to lease land in a little-used corner of the campus, giving birth to Stanford's Industrial Park.

The late 1930's saw the beginning of another Stanford collaboration that had major significance in the development of the university's ties with local industry. Frederick E. Terman, the son of Stanford psychology professor Lewis M. Terman, had joined the Stanford faculty in 1925; he headed the electrical engineering department from 1937 until he was named Dean of Engineering in 1944. In 1939, he encouraged two former students, William Hewlett and David Packard, to remain in the area to start their electronics collaboration in a Palo Alto garage. He then helped find the first customer, Disney Productions, for their innovative oscillator. In 1956, the highly successful Hewlett-Packard Company would move its headquarters to the Stanford Industrial Park. Terman continued to play a crucial role in fostering closer ties between Stanford and high-technology industries as dean and later as university provost.

A much different legacy was given to the university in 1938 by Dean of Education Ellwood P. Cubberley. Cubberley had arrived at Stanford in 1898, a young assistant professor. When he was appointed head of the Education Department two months later, President Jordan warned him that the department was in disrepute and he had three years to make it respectable. Not only did he succeed in building a strong department and later school of education, he carefully invested his own earnings from writing and editing. Shortly after his retirement in 1933, Dean and Mrs. Cubberley gave the university stocks and bonds valued at $367,000 for new quarters for the School of Education. The Education Building, housing classrooms, offices, Cubberley Auditorium, and the Cubberley Library, was dedicated in 1938. Later contributions to the university would bring his total gift to more than $770,000. As a professor, Cubberley's annual salary had peaked at only $8,000.

As campus commentators described the recovery from economic troubles and sought to combat the country club image, many, especially alumni, also worried about the loss of traditions associated with turn-of-the-century Stanford—among them the "hello" tradition, which required those traversing the Quad to greet whomever they passed. This reflection of the easy congeniality of the small student body of the 1890's was little remembered by students now numbering over eight times those of 1900, whizzing past the Quad in Ford roadsters.

In 1940, members of the ASSU Executive Committee concluded that it was time to do something about campus moaning for "the good old days" at Stanford. "Back-to-the-Farm Week" was their answer. Bill Turner, chairman of the festivities, explained, "During these three days, the Stanford student body—and it is hoped the faculty—will re-live past Farm history." For the first day, jeans, ginghams, derbies, and corncob pipes were recommended. Although costumes were not compulsory, a vigilante committee headed by Gordy "No-Gun" Nicoll threatened to "jug" those not in proper costumes in a wooden jail in front of the library. Other activities included a beard-growing contest, the second annual Boathouse Day and barbecue, and the elimination of cars from campus for a day. Executive Committee member Jack Alltucker noted, "People here are getting stuck up and snobbish, driv-

faculty sought to provide a forum for student discussion through courses and through such activities as the 1938 Peace Day, which closed with roundtable discussions of controversial aspects of peace and war—the benefits of collective security and trade agreements and the impact of totalitarianism, imperialism, and propaganda. Responding to a request from the federal government to major universities, a 1940 faculty committee, chaired by engineering dean Samuel

ing around in their big cars with their noses in the air. It would be good to get the ties off them for a while. This is getting to be a rich man's school—you can't deny it."[10]

But as the 1930's drew to a close, front-page headlines about the Back-to-the-Farm Movement or the latest ups and downs of Stanford football were routinely joined by war news from Europe as Germany occupied Austria, Czechoslovakia, Belgium, Holland, Poland, and then France. Although American sentiment still was largely against involvement in another European war, the American government was sending food and arms to a badly shaken Britain, and popular feeling lay increasingly on the side of the Allies.

Faculty members were keenly aware of the growing trauma in Europe throughout the Depression years as colleagues were forced to emigrate from highly respected European universities and as research was diverted for military purposes or stifled altogether. The

B. Morris, suggested to the administration ways in which Stanford might contribute to American defense and a presumed upcoming war effort.

Yet unlike the era before American entry into World War I, when three years of Stanford interest in Belgian relief and the volunteer ambulance services to France prepared the community for the changes to come, the campus of 1940 remained insulated from war. Graduates, instead, would speak of memories of the beauty of the hills in the spring, or Memorial Church silhouetted in the sunset, of gatherings at the Cellar and the dash to the City after Big Game, of the warmth and intimacy of college friendships and the excitement of sharing ideas with a friendly faculty. Few could have suspected that the Second World War would bring about a transition in the university's ambitions and its academic and community life greater than any change yet experienced.

Fewer students could afford cameras during the Depression, but accomplished student photographers joined the staffs of the "Daily" and the "Quad."

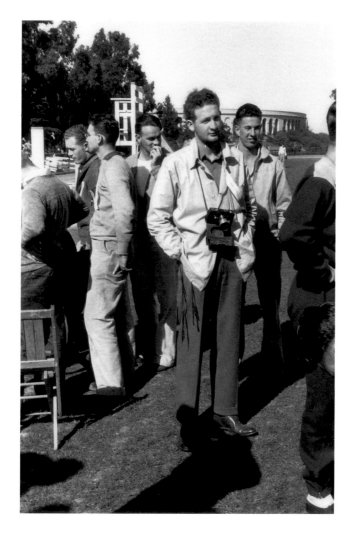

Collegiate style: in a picture posed for a 1929 Chrysler advertisement, Stanford males hold on to the legacy of informality with cords, flannel shirts, and Stanford "match-scratcher" belt buckles. Below, a 1939 fashion pose at the new Lagunita boathouse.

Even in candid shots, Stanford's students begin to sport the new, more formal collegiate style. Long-standing tradition, inaccurately attributed to Mrs. Stanford, dictated that women must wear silk stockings on the Quad.

The Post Office, where waits at General Delivery for letters and laundry sent back from home are long and congenial.

Relief from studying comes in many ways: a 1938 South Sea Islands party at the Medical School and a humorous sendoff to a 1934 graduate.

The "motor boys" of Beta Theta Pi, about 1937.

Toyon Hall study, perhaps tidied up a bit for the photographer.

A 1931 "Kaffee Klatch" at Roble Gym on University Day, a day of visits and open houses.

Student body president Kenneth Cuthbertson, '40, and vice-president Coline Upshaw, '40 (the future Mrs. Cuthbertson), dress up for Back-to-the-Farm Day in their senior year.

Behind Encina, a student shows off his English "kiddie car," an Austin Swallow. More typical four-wheel transportation stands behind students at right.

Tapping a keg at a beer bust in the hills.

Olive trees from the Menlo Park estate of Stanford trustee Timothy Hopkins are transplanted in front of newly built Memorial Hall, autumn 1937.

233

Cars of every vintage share parking in front of Encina.

Many students still "earned while they learned": Joe Davis collecting for his 1930 laundry service in Encina Hall.

The heyday of both the Greek system and eating clubs: Kappa Kappa Gamma on Lasuen mid-decade and El Cuadro's dining hall at 3 Encina Commons in 1933.

In 1930, the women's and men's councils assumed oversight of the university's increasingly complex code of student conduct.

The smell of coffee, cocoa, and doughnuts at the Cellar, located in the basement of the Men's Clubhouse, lives in the memories of generations of students.

The Stanford Union, flanked by the Women's and Men's Clubhouses served as campus social and political center. The public dining room became a faculty favorite.

Members of the class of '98 gather in 1930 for a photograph on the spacious lawn of Lou Henry Hoover, '98, following lunch across the street at the home of Parnie Hamilton Storey, '98.

"Pajamarino," dating back to a nightshirt parade at a baseball rally in the 1980's, continues as a popular campus dance.

The collapse of part of the Lagunita boathouse in 1938, captured on film by "Daily" photographer Jeannette Hill, '39, was featured in "Life" magazine.

Stanford women, long out of bloomers, enjoy the California sunshine: celebrating the new Lagunita Boathouse, 1939; waiting for a race in the waters of Lagunita in 1938; picnicking out at the coast; bicycling near Los Altos mid-decade; and sunbathing along the Row.

The Vow Boys swore they would never lose to USC and threw California into the bargain. They turned around Stanford football with a 25-4-2 varsity record between 1933 and 1935 and played in three Rose Bowls.

Two Stanford All-Americas, Jim Lawson, '25 (left), and Bobby Grayson, '36, were on the coaching staff of Tiny Thornhill (in hat).

The kids' gate at Stanford stadium, 1940.

The Stanford rooting section salutes its favorite sons in 1935.

Some of the Immortal 21, who recaptured the Axe from Berkeley in April 1930, including ringleader Donald J. Kropp (at front in sweater), '26, law '31.

The 1938 basketball team (far right) on its way to New York to play Long Island and City College of New York. The previous winter the team shocked the East Coast by stopping Long Island's 43-game winning streak.

Dubbed the "laughing boys" by New York sports writers because of their unorthodox, free-wheeling style of play, the basketball teams of the three Luisetti years won 68 games and lost only 12.

Angelo "Hank" Luisetti, '38, dunks the ball. Luisetti's innovative running one-handed jump shot from anywhere on the floor changed basketball forever. His no. 7 was retired.

Tom Cordry, Stanford forward and 1933 team captain, was also senior class president. "His whirlwind trickiness," said the "Quad," "made him a favorite with the fans."

Luisetti took a shot at Hollywood movie making in Paramount's 1939 Betty Grable film, "Campus Confessions."

August "Gus" Meier, '35, world-record hurdler, sits on the judge's stand at Angell Field with coach "Dink" Templeton.

Ernest P. "Husky" Hunt, seen here filming a discus throw by Stanley Anderson, '35, coached a wide range of sports in his 33-year Stanford career.

Benjamin "Blazing Ben" Eastman, '33, in a relay finish. During two weeks of the 1932 season, Eastman set world marks in the 440- and 880-yard runs.

Lawson Little (right), '34, and Charles Seaver, '34, at the clubhouse of the new Stanford golf course. Little won the British and U.S. Amateur championships in 1934 and the U.S. Open in 1940. Seaver was co-medalist in the 1931 U.S. Amateur and was on the Walker Cup Team in 1932.

Stanford's Sunken Diamond was completed in 1931, and that same season the Cardinal won the California Intercollegiate Baseball Association title.

Equestrian activities are a natural for The Farm, especially with mounts available from the ROTC cavalry unit.

One of the polo team members bore a famous name— Will Rogers Jr., '35 (second from left), was also an intercollegiate debater.

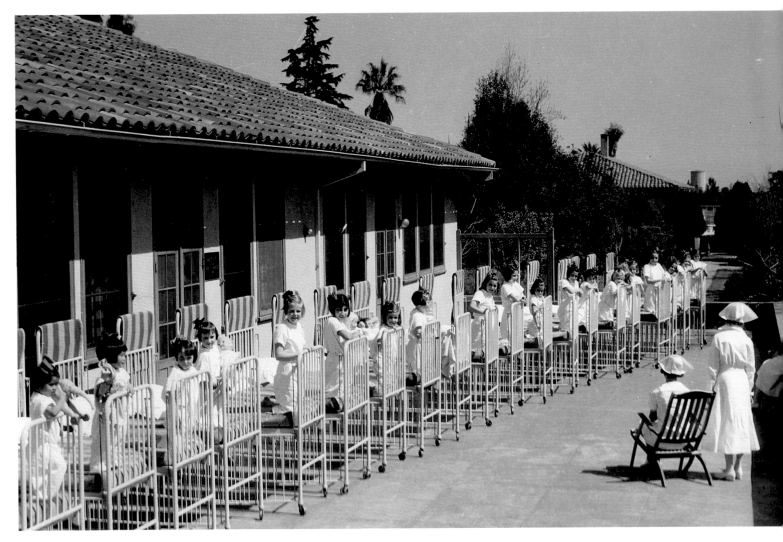

Children, many from San Francisco, enjoy the Palo Alto sun at the Stanford Convalescent Home.

A portion of the Stanford family home, salvaged after the 1906 earthquake, served the Con Home into the 1960's.

At the Con Home Labor Day, students grapple with the vegetable patch.

Student-directed fundraising drives provide valuable support to the Con Home. Jim Ludlam, '36, accepts donations during a 1936 stunt featuring an elephant loaned at the last minute by Barnes's five-ring Circus.

251

At Back-to-the-Farm days in November 1940, students celebrated the pioneer era with their own version of a rougher Stanford.

An alternative method of transportation during Back-to-the-Farm.

A banner advertises just a few of the many activities of the day in 1941.

The Stanford Geological Survey of 1932 explores the northern end of the Humbolt Range in Nevada.

Auto shop provides hands-on experience in mechanical engineering.

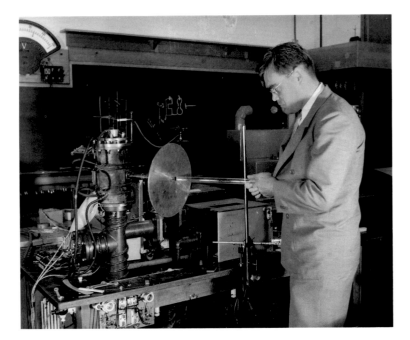

Physicist William W. Hansen's discoveries in the laboratory of the Physics Department, as well as his theoretical studies, led to key developments in the acceleration of electrons.

Biology students in their lab high in Jordan Hall on the Outer Quad.

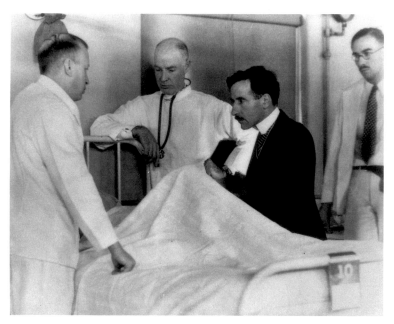

Dr. George DeForest Barnett (with stethoscope), famed for his teaching of physical diagnosis, is joined in ward rounds by Dr. Leo Eloesser, clinical professor of surgery (in suit), and two interns at the Medical School's Lane Hospital in San Francisco.

Renaissance scholar and dramatist Margery Bailey poses for a Christmas card reenactment of "The Angels Appearing to the Shepherds" from a Flemish book of hours.

A student artist is captured by the lens.

Botanist Ira Wiggins, whose field research stretched from Alaska to the Galápagos, watches as students complete lab exercises.

The concentration, and exhaustion, of studying and exams caught the eye of "Daily" photographer Tro Harper, '37—and belied Stanford's country club image of the 1930's.

*Filing into the new Frost
Amphitheater is the class of
'37, the first to receive diplomas there.*

The laying of senior class plaques began with the "almost pioneer" class of '96, which placed its plaque front and center of Memorial Church. Senior class president David D. Ryus III (left) and Jack H. Laney pose with President Wilbur in 1939.

The Stanfords' farm in 1937: beyond the shining fender, hay is harvested with Board of Athletic Control equipment; in the distance is the University Library.

*The flurry of exams and of a commencement soon to come can
be left behind in the evening tranquillity of Lagunita.*

We must work unremittingly to maintain a university of true distinction, to foster at Stanford tolerance and understanding, to preserve and defend our precious freedoms in a tortured, war-crazed world.   DONALD B. TRESIDDER, *1941*

W ar news mingled with Stanford's golden jubilee throughout 1941, broadening the celebration from nostalgia for pioneer days to a reflection on the efficacy of American higher education in the coming world crisis. Midway through the year, a four-day commemorative symposium, "The University and the Future of America," featured major speakers in education, science, and business who could not help but call attention to the impact of the war in Europe and the current challenge to higher education.

On the last day of the conference, June 20, the new Hoover Tower was dedicated. The original Hoover War Library, founded in 1919 by trustee Herbert Hoover, had outgrown its quarters in the main library as its extraordinary collection expanded—newspapers, government documents, correspondence, secret diaries, propaganda leaflets, and other rare materials— documenting the coming of wars and revolutions and suggesting routes to peace.

As the June conference ended, a new carillon of 35 bells rang out from the tower, the gift of Belgian universities and foundations to honor Herbert Hoover's work as director of Belgian relief from 1914 to 1919. Two days later, in violation of a treaty between the two countries, Germany invaded Russia; the war took on a new, larger dimension, and American intervention seemed all the more inevitable.

"Hitler or no Hitler, war or no war," stated chemistry professor Robert E. Swain, chairman of the golden jubilee, the climactic celebration of Stanford's opening day would go on. Five days of events were held, starting on October 1 with reenactment of the opening ceremony of 1891 on the Quad. Yet even in this celebration, the war was not far away. A dramatic masque, "The Winds of Freedom Blow," written by drama professor Norman Philbrick, was presented at the black-tie dinner in the Palace Hotel's Garden Court in San Francisco. Students, alumni, and faculty made up the corps of actors, singing and speaking choruses in a moving dramatization of the university's motto, centering on the closing of the University of Leiden earlier that year by German forces occupying the Netherlands.

The evening's speaker, Raymond B. Fosdick, president of the Rockefeller Foundation and an important supporter of Stanford's drive for research support, also took "Die Luft der Freiheit weht" as his theme and spoke of the need to protect intellectual freedom. Stanford was young compared with Leiden, Oxford, or the University of Paris. But if, by Stanford's centennial in 1991, "liberty has been reestablished in places where now it is gone, if democracy is a living, growing force, it will be in no small part because institutions like Stanford have led the way to new light and have dared to dream of greater days to come," said Fosdick.[1]

Despite anxiety over the future, or perhaps because of it, life continued with fall's traditional menu: the Big Game bonfire, Gaieties, and Pajamarino were great successes. Football made the headlines as Washington's Huskies attacked and Santa Clara's Broncos invaded. Then the Axe was lost to Cal, and along with it Rose Bowl hopes, in the November football classic.

With defense industries monopolizing supplies of silk and nylon, tradition bit the Inner Quad dust once again when the Women's Council approved bobby socks as an appropriate alternative to stockings worn by women on the Quad. Along with the socks—pale pastels with monograms preferred—came long hair in braids, leather moccasins, and the single 60-inch strand of pearls. *Daily* reporter Aimie Reichart, usually known for her columns on details of the war, noted in a brief fashion statement that Stanford's coeds were like those at any other college, "well-groomed, long-maned, well-tailored and studiedly sloppy."[2]

The campus settled down to an end-of-the-quarter study drive, but on December 7 news came of the Japanese attack on the American naval base in Hawaii. Californians braced themselves for invasion as the next target in the Japanese offensive. They were keenly aware of being unprepared, mentally as well as militarily, for a major Pacific war. "And so we were at war and we tried to think that books and classes were important and we kept right on with our work," wrote "Bull Session" columnist Cheslie Saroyan a few days later in the *Daily*. "We were all very surprised at the speed and power of the Japanese, and we couldn't understand how the islands were left unprotected like they were and how it was possible for the Japanese to get so close."[3] Rumors were rife about Japanese planes on their way to San Francisco. Conversation was grim and determined, sounding reminiscent of news reports of London during the Blitz.

An all-university assembly of students, faculty, and staff gathered in Memorial Auditorium. Ray Lyman

Wilbur was blunt. "You can well realize we have had a very heavy blow in the Pacific. We are in a hole. The British are in a hole, and our difficulties are going to increase instead of decrease. Whether we have any mastery at all in the Pacific is yet to be shown." Wilbur encouraged students to stay at Stanford as long as they could and stressed the value of education to the war effort. "Be reluctant to drop out of the University. The government will pull you out if it wants you. An engineering student who can get a new idea that will make an airplane go twenty miles faster per hour is worth a hundred thousand men in uniform." He ended the assembly with a plea for tolerance toward Japanese-American students as fellow members of the Stanford community.[4]

Spurred by news stories of the bombings of London and Shanghai, civil defense was quickly organized. Stanford's Civilian Defense Committee faced the problem of blacking out 1,500 acres of campus in the event of an air-raid alarm—not only for the protection of civilian residents but because Stanford lights could guide enemy planes to the nearby air base at Moffett Field and to the vitally important Permanente magnesium and cement plant in the hills behind Los Altos. Volunteer units were organized to help with possible fires and injuries, to help the police, and to serve as "watch officers." Three days after Pearl Harbor, the Stanford community had its first drill, and the campus went black in three minutes.

While classes continued, students entered the home-front campaign with fervor: they bought war stamps to help the government build jeeps, gave blood to the Red Cross, saved junk for salvage drives, entertained soldiers, sponsored consumer education efforts, and set up scholarships through war bonds for soldiers who would one day return from the war.

Bailey Willis, the gingery, bewhiskered emeritus geology professor, turned the bagging of 64,000 pounds of Monterey sand for home defense into a competition among four fraternities. One team peaked at three bags a minute, and 2,000 bags were filled and ready for distribution to every house on campus.

By early 1942, Stanford faculty members were called on by the government for a variety of tasks, among them an education campaign aimed at informing Americans, long accustomed to tracking the European war, about the many distinct cultures of the Pacific. "It was difficult for many of the soldiers from such states as Tennessee and Mississippi to grasp the intricate social and racial problems of the peoples of the Pacific area," reported Wilbur, just returned from lecturing at Army training camps up and down the West Coast. "The citizens of other parts of our country are looking to us here on the Coast to know something of the facts and of the peoples involved."[5] Stanford had a long tradition of teaching and research about the history, art, biology, and geology of nations bordering the Pacific, placing it in a special position to contribute to national understanding.

Shortly after Pearl Harbor, the Japanese Student Association wrote Wilbur that "as American citizens of Japanese ancestry, we have been prepared to assume and discharge our duties and responsibilities yet little did we dream that we would be called upon to prove our loyalty under the circumstances in which we now find ourselves. Realizing the necessity of unity in the critical period ahead, we pledge our full support in the present emergency."[6] But by May 1942, fewer than a dozen Japanese-American students were still at Stanford. Some had transferred to midwestern colleges; those who remained were seniors, holding out in their last quarter to receive their diplomas. On May 23, Executive Order 9066, calling for the internment of all Japanese and all American citizens of Japanese descent, caught up with the Stanford campus. An evacuation order was unceremoniously tacked on a telephone pole in front of the Japanese clubhouse on Santa Ynez Street. The remaining students were sent by train to the Santa Anita Assembly Center, a converted race track in Southern California. That same month, Japanese history professor Yamato Ichihashi, approaching retirement after a long career at Stanford, was interned with his family at Manzanar. He was quickly granted a leave of absence, and his campus property was watched over by his colleague, historian Payson Treat.

Commencement now would be filled with men in military uniforms, who received their commissions as well as their degrees. Many, called up during the year, received their diplomas in absentia. Male enrollment was dropping fast, and the ratio of men to women fell below 2 to 1 for the first time in decades. The normally passive student interest in ROTC changed dramatically as men faced the impending draft call. Math and engineering classes were overflowing, language and current affairs courses suddenly popular. Engagement and wedding announcements seemed to appear daily.

The war effort—and the military—soon dominated campus life. Under the Army Specialized Training Program (ASTP), a federal program designed to use college and university facilities to train specialists for the war effort, the first soldier-students arrived at Stanford in the spring of 1943. Other smaller military programs joined ASTP: Army and Navy medical training programs, programs for the retraining and reassignment of officers, programs in industrial management and drafting for those who would remain on the home front. The president's residence on the Knoll was lent to the Army to house Women's Army Corps (WAC) trainees participating in the special physical therapy school. By June, nearly 2,400 soldiers were registered in intensive course work in engineering, language and area studies, psychology, and premedicine, with the number jumping to almost 3,000 by fall quarter. That same fall quarter saw more than 1,000 regularly enrolled men and 1,460 women students. With more than 5,000 students, the university's enrollment had reached an all-time high.

Classes operated on both a regular and a "swing shift" schedule, with lights burning in Quad class-

rooms until 11:30 P.M. Yet many faculty members were called up for military posts and wartime research—such as electrical engineering professor Frederick E. Terman, who had gathered some eighteen Stanford alumni to work with him at the Radio Research Laboratory in Cambridge, and physicist William Hansen, working sixteen-hour days directing radar research simultaneously at MIT's Radiation Laboratory in Cambridge and with Sperry Gyroscope Company on Long Island. William F. Durand, the nationally known 84-year-old emeritus professor of aeronautics and an accomplished linguist, found himself back in Washington, D.C., with the National Advisory Committee for Aeronautics and the National Research Council. Those faculty members remaining covered a heavy load of teaching, often to soldier-students comparatively ill-prepared by the Army for college coursework, in addition to research. The chaplain taught trigonometry; a music professor taught engineering drawing. Emeriti were recalled to active duty to teach and to direct engineering and scientific research.

Soldiers filled the dormitories and most fraternity houses; the regularly enrolled men—greatly reduced in numbers—lived in the remaining fraternities. The men in khaki became an integral part of Stanford life. "It's a long way from the 'country club' Stanford of a few years ago," reported senior Patricia Clary to alumni readers in the *Stanford Alumni Review*. "The Stanford of today is a community unmarked by the rah-rah, the Del Monte week-end, the snobbery, and the display of wealth which, rightly or wrongly, were

popularly thought to characterize it."[7] Nonetheless, the Nitery, little used during the 1930's as a social gathering spot, came into its own for dancing and live entertainment almost nightly.

Just as during the First World War, women moved into positions of student leadership. A change in the ASSU constitution was required to allow vice president Janet McClanahan, '44, to take over from president Jack Reynolds, '44, when he was inducted into

the Army. "Lipsticked cigarette butts" littered the floor of the *Daily* Shack as women gathered and edited campus news and flaunted tradition by painting the walls and bringing in ashtrays and wastebaskets.

The visibility and concerns of the women on campus led to yet another review of the sorority system, capping a controversy that had been debated and fought for decades. In the spring of 1943, Roble's student sponsors (those highly influential senior women selected from among the student body—hall and sorority—as advisors and monitors of the freshmen women at Roble) demanded that the Board of Trustees eliminate sororities at Stanford.

Stanford's nine sororities were a success story markedly different from campus fraternities. Scholarship records were uniformly high, and chapters paid their bills. They were extremely popular and prestigious on campus. They were also increasingly selective, as the number of women more than tripled from the original 500 and the number of chapter houses remained the same. Indignant parents blamed university staff when heartbroken daughters were not pledged. Hall women complained of the commotion caused by the frenzy of spring rushing, the exaggerated glamour, and the elitist atmosphere that fostered social distinctions based on wealth. Student leaders and dean's office staff saw an artificial and destructive

wedge between Stanford's women, noting that while some 90 percent expressed a desire to pledge, only about 16 percent—some 270 women of over 1,500—could actually do so.

The administration had hesitated to deal directly with the conflict until provoked by the student petitions, backed by the Dean of Women. A special trustee committee spent another year debating the issue. Surprisingly, the lines for and against sororities were not simply divided along house-hall membership. Some chapter members were adamantly in favor of the sorority system, others equally against it. Dean Mary Yost, herself an alumna of Kappa Alpha Theta, came down squarely on the side of elimination.

In April 1944, the Board of Trustees voted to disband Stanford's sororities because of excessive competition leading to "serious disunity" between sorority and hall women. By the end of the academic year, chapter houses were turned over to the university, and supervision and ownership of all women's housing unified under the university.

Although some vocal alumni feared that the ultimate motive was to eliminate fraternities as well, the men's houses remained unaffected by the debate. They were an entrenched part of campus life but did not monopolize campus prestige or political power. Hall men, especially from Encina, dominated ASSU and held key positions on student publications. Many of Stanford's men were not interested in or attracted to fraternity life, finding more than adequate visibility and pride in club and dorm associations. Even sorority women rarely distinguished between men of the hall and the Row, dating both with equal zest.

Nor did the university seem anxious to control male student behavior by taking over operation of fraternities, even though competition between fraternities and hall men could erupt in violence unheard of among the women, such as the accidental death in 1941 of a Beta Theta Pi member who fell off the Beta house roof during a melee with freshmen from Encina. Independence and competition among the men were considered essential parts of their college experience. On the other hand, the independence and influence of the sororities challenged university control over women undergraduates. The 1944 ruling of the trustees was specifically aimed at bringing women fully under the wing of the university socially, academically, and financially.

In 1940, President Wilbur had reached the retirement age of 65 set for faculty and senior administrative staff, but, at the request of the Trustees, he twice agreed to stay on—first to preside at the University's fiftieth anniversary celebration and then to ease the transition of the campus to wartime conditions. Meanwhile, Board president Donald B. Tresidder was entrusted with compiling a new list of candidates. The Alumni Association was asked, faculty were queried, and interviews were conducted. The final choice was remarkably close to home: Tresidder himself, A.B. '19, M.D. '27.

As president of Yosemite Park and Curry Company, Tresidder was an experienced businessman rather than an academic. Nevertheless, he was closely associated with Stanford as alumnus, volunteer, and trustee. "Dr. Tresidder is a Stanford man. He has stood in line at the General Delivery window. He has learned about the spirit of sportsmanship from Harry Maloney. He has hashed for Mrs. Green and has shouted himself hoarse giving the 'Axe' yell at Big

Game. He put himself through Stanford and knows her and what she represents."[8] The Stanford community was impressed with this tall, spare, and very friendly man, who had directed much of his own time since 1939 to Stanford's welfare.

When Tresidder became university president in the fall of 1943, the campus faced major housing shortages for both students and government personnel, as well as a curriculum and a physical plant that were overwhelmed by the goals of the war effort. Two-thirds of the student body were soldiers in intensive coursework, and classes were running around the clock and throughout the year.

Yet, as the war wound down, Stanford faced an equally unsettling transformation with the sudden removal of almost 3,000 soldier-students. As early as February 1944, when the Army announced that it was cutting back ASTP enrollments, Tresidder had to quiet fears about the sudden loss of federal support: "It has been a real satisfaction to the administration and faculty to feel that we were making a direct contribution to the war effort. Our real business is not training men for war but training young people for peace. We'll go on with our original business."[9]

Tresidder was not able to see his clarion call fulfilled. His untimely death of a heart attack in 1948 prevented him from seeing Stanford move into national prominence, buoyed by national economic prosperity, heightened public interest in higher education, the availability of major federal funding for university research, and the swelling ranks of supportive Stanford alumni and friends. It would fall to the post-war campus—to the new faculty and students, administration, and alumni—to oversee Stanford's transition into a university of international stature.

At Stanford's fiftieth anniversary celebration in autumn 1941, trustee Herbert Hoover listens as Ray Lyman Wilbur addresses the crowd in Inner Quad.

A new physical presence on campus, Hoover Tower can be seen beyond Encina.

With United States entry into World War II, the armed services become a major part of campus life: men of the Army Specialized Training Program (ASTP) at History Corner.

ASTP drill on Panama Street, near the site of today's Mitchell Earth Sciences building.

Officers of state and community defense organizations in western states attending a War Department civilian defense school were assigned to Sequoia Hall (in distance). Tents used as gas chambers and gas masks are part of the two-week course.

In fall 1943, ASTP soldiers drill in Stanford stadium, one of the many athletic facilities turned over to the Army.

Electrical engineering Professor William G. Hoover (at left) with engineering students of the ASTP program.

Shau Wing Chan, professor of Chinese and humanities, instructs a student in the ASTP area and languages unit, 1944.

Students join the war effort by selling war bonds and underwriting construction of jeeps like this "Peep I" through purchase of war stamps.

The Japanese Student Association sits for a group portrait
with President Wilbur and professor of Japanese history
Yamato Ichihashi. Although they offered their services to the
university after Pearl Harbor, most, including Professor
Ichihashi, were interned or left for midwestern colleges.

For the first time in Stanford history, women students outnumber the regularly enrolled men: by two to one by 1944.

Lagunita Court dining hall is filled with women residents and hashers.

In a dramatic clash between the philosophies of dormitory and sorority life, women students successfully petitioned for university takeover of sorority houses. By 1945, all Stanford women live in university-run residences like the Union dormitory or former sorority houses. Theresa Russell House had been Kappa Kappa Gamma.

The car remains an important part of Stanford life.

With silk and nylon given up for the war effort, style goes casual: sweaters, bobby socks, saddle shoes, loafers —and even jeans.

Although fraternity houses are now largely taken over by soldiers, fraternity life continues in its own lively fashion.

The second floor of the old fire house was home to a small but sturdy band of students who answered the deafening fire whistle along with the pros.

Hashing is still a much-sought-after job for the working student—with convenient hours and free board.

Superintendent of Athletic Facilities E. B. "Sam" McDonald's
victory garden at the Convalescent Home produces both
vegetables and fun for the children.

Fashion finds an unlikely home in the pages of the "Chaparral" as two coeds model for photographer Bill Hyer, '44.

During the war years, women took on a larger role in politics, drama, and publishing, but life continued as usual in the library and on the sun porch.

Though the athletic program had come to a standstill, students gathered at Yosemite for a favorite Stanford winter sport.

Many of the women learned skiing from physical education professor Luell Weed Guthrie.

The glamour of military aviation sparks interest in Stanford's Flying Club.

The 1944 production "Is Life Worth Living" in modern dress contrasts with Molière's "A School for Husbands" of the same year.

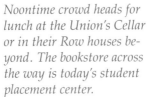

Noontime crowd heads for lunch at the Union's Cellar or in their Row houses beyond. The bookstore across the way is today's student placement center.

Emeritus faculty and their wives gather with President Wilbur in 1943, the year he retired as Stanford's leader.

President Donald B. Tresidder, who succeeded Wilbur in 1943, and his wife, Mary Curry Tresidder, were licensed pilots who flew their own plane for business and pleasure.

A quiet lane in the Arboretum, where trees have reached maturity during the university's first 50 years.

Reference Matter

Notes

Consult the Suggested Readings for bibliographical information on works not cited in full in these notes.

CHAPTER 1

1. Jane Stanford to Leland Stanford, Nov. 17, 1880. Jane L. Stanford Papers, Stanford University Archives.
2. *New York Herald*, Mar. 22, 1885. Stanford Family Scrapbooks, Stanford University Archives.
3. Jane Stanford, July 19, 1892, journal entry sent to David Starr Jordan in 1897. Jane L. Stanford Papers, Stanford University Archives.
4. Charles W. Eliot to David Starr Jordan, June 26, 1919. David Starr Jordan Papers, Stanford University Archives.
5. Ibid.
6. *New York Commercial Advertiser*, [1885]. Stanford Family Scrapbooks, Stanford University Archives.
7. *Stanford University: The Founding Grant*, IX.1.
8. *San Francisco Examiner*, Apr. 17, 1889.
9. David Starr Jordan, *The Days of a Man*, pp. 355–56.
10. *San Francisco Examiner*, Mar. 29, 1891.
11. David Starr Jordan to John Casper Branner, May 17, 1891. J. C. Branner Papers, Stanford University Archives.
12. Ibid.

CHAPTER 2

1. Ellen Coit Elliott, *It Happened This Way*, p. 179.
2. Orrin Leslie Elliott, *Stanford University: The First Twenty-Five Years*, p. ix.
3. Leland Stanford, *Exercises of the Opening Day, October 1, 1891*, pp. 11–12. Stanford University Archives.
4. David Starr Jordan, "Evolution of the College Curriculum," in his *Science Sketches* (Chicago: A. C. McClurg & Co., 1888).
5. Quoted in Edith Mirrielees, *Stanford Mosaic*, p. 119.
6. O. L. Elliott, *Stanford University*, p. 86.
7. David Starr Jordan, "Woman and the University," in his *The Voice of the Scholar* (San Francisco: Paul Elder & Co., 1903), pp. 192, 196.
8. Jane L. Stanford to David Starr Jordan. David Starr Jordan Papers, Stanford University Archives.
9. Quoted in O. L. Elliott, *Stanford University*, p. 140.

CHAPTER 3

1. Leo Stanley, "Via Stanford to San Quentin," in Mirrielees, *Stanford Mosaic*, p. 45.
2. Ray Lyman Wilbur, *The Memoirs of Ray Lyman Wilbur, 1875–1949*, p. 122.
3. Edith Mirrielees, *Stanford: The Story of a University*, p. 125.
4. William James, "The Development of Stanford's Ideal Destiny," Founders Day Address, Mar. 1906. Stanford University Archives.

5. Edith Mirrielees, "The Day After," *Stanford Alumnus*, May 1906, p. 7.
6. *Daily Palo Alto*, Apr. 21, 1906. A rich source of eyewitness accounts can be found in the Stanford Earthquake Collection, SC206, Stanford University Archives.
7. David Starr Jordan to Andrew White, Apr. 24, 1906. David Starr Jordan Papers, Stanford University Archives.
8. Bruce Bliven, "The Innocent Decade," in Mirrielees, *Stanford Mosaic*, p. 58.
9. Frank Hill, "Yes, But I DON'T WANT TO," in Mirrielees, *Stanford Mosaic*, p. 77.
10. Bliven, "Innocent Decade," p. 57.
11. Wilbur, *Memoirs*, p. 34.
12. *Leland Stanford Junior University Fifth Register*, 1895–1896, p. 25.
13. O. L. Elliott, *Stanford University*, p. 408.
14. Benjamin Ide Wheeler to David Starr Jordan, May 3, 1911. David Starr Jordan Papers, Stanford University Archives.
15. John Casper Branner to David Starr Jordan, Jan. 1, 1914. David Starr Jordan Papers, Stanford University Archives.
16. David Starr Jordan to John Casper Branner, July 29, 1915. Herbert Hoover Pre-Commerce Papers, Hoover Institution Archives.

CHAPTER 4

1. *Stanford Illustrated Review*, Sept. 1916, p. 6.
2. Wilbur, *Memoirs*, p. 217. For an excellent discussion of late nineteenth- and early twentieth-century reform of curriculum and college life, see Helen Lefkowitz Horowitz, *Campus Life: Undergraduate Cultures from the End of the Eighteenth Century to the Present* (New York: Knopf, 1987).
3. Ray Lyman Wilbur, Aug. 5, 1916, quoted in his *Annual Report of the University for the Twenty-Fifth Academic Year* (Stanford, Calif.: Stanford University, 1916), pp. 21–22.
4. Ibid., pp. 19–20.
5. *Stanford Alumnus*, Apr. 1917, p. 264.
6. *Stanford University Bulletin: Thirty-Third Annual Register* (Stanford, Calif.: Stanford University, 1923), p. 158. The demise of "Western Civilization" during the late 1960's was one of many curriculum and institutional changes brought about by the three-year Study of Education at Stanford (SES). In 1980 the requirement returned as "Western Culture" with a menu of course options; in 1989 it was changed to "Cultures, Ideas, and Values," with greater emphasis on the contributions of women, minorities, and non-Western cultures.
7. *San Francisco Bulletin*, July 22, 1889.

CHAPTER 5

1. *Stanford Daily*, May 19, 1930.
2. *Stanford Daily*, May 13, 1933. In 1973, the university

once again successfully petitioned the Santa Clara County
Superior Court for a change in Mrs. Stanford's amendment
to the Founding Grant and succeeded in removing all refer-
ence to quotas on enrollment.

3. "Toyon Formal Will Be Novel," *Stanford Daily*, Feb. 8,
1932, p. 1.

4. "Views of Life Expounded by Leading Stanfordites,"
Stanford Daily, May 26, 1933, p. 1.

5. *Time* 17, no. 23 (June 8, 1931): 40.

6. E. R. Embree, "In order of their eminence, an ap-
praisal of American universities," *Atlantic Monthly* 152 (June
1935): 652–64; also reported in *Newsweek*, June 22, 1935, p.
15.

7. *ASSU Handbook*, Stanford University, 1930, p. 106.

8. *Chaparral*, Jan. 1931, p. 16.

9. *Stanford Quad*, 1930, p. 53.

10. "Good old days," *Stanford Daily*, Feb. 27, 1940; "Ex-
com approves," *Stanford Daily*, Jan. 17, 1940.

CHAPTER 6

1. *Stanford Alumni Review*, Oct. 1941, p. 9.
2. *Stanford Daily*, Sept. 22, 1941, p. 3.
3. *Stanford Daily*, Dec. 10, 1941, p. 4.
4. *Stanford Daily*, Dec. 10, 1941, p. 1.
5. *Stanford Alumni Review*, Apr. 1942, p.1.
6. *Stanford Daily*, Dec. 10, 1941, p.4.
7. *Stanford Alumni Review*, Nov. 1943, p. 8.
8. *Stanford Daily*, Jan. 25, 1943, p. 4.
9. *Stanford Alumni Review*, Mar. 1944, p. 1.

Suggested Readings

THE UNIVERSITY

The archival record of the Stanford community—letters
and diaries, committee minutes, reports and other official
records, monographs and journal articles, photographs,
ephemeral publications, and scrapbooks—is voluminous
and provides a wealth of material for study. The collection is
available to the public in the Stanford University Archives.

Unfortunately, few analytical accounts of Stanford community life exist outside the realm of dissertations. Works
written by those inside the community are rarely critical and
are as much a reflection of the community image as they are
a source of information. Works by authors looking in from
the outside, in turn, are superficial and rarely understand
Stanford's philosophical foundations and intrinsically Western nature. However, the following works provide background useful to any study of the Stanford community from
1885 to 1945.

Allen, Peter C. *Stanford: From the Foothills to the Bay* (Stan-
    ford: Stanford Historical Society / Stanford Alumni Asso-
    ciation, 1980), 228 pp. This well-written and colorful
    overview of Stanford, past and present, is aimed at the
    general public and summarizes notable points in Stan-
    ford's history, including faculty accomplishments and the
    development of schools and departments.

Cavalli, Gary, *Stanford Sports* (Stanford: Stanford Alumni As-
    sociation, 1982), 224 pp. The large format and color pho-
    tographs overshadow a readable and balanced history of
    men's and women's sports of all kinds. Includes a very
    useful listing of Stanford athletic awards and records.

Elliott, Ellen Coit, *It Happened This Way* (Stanford: Stanford
    University Press, 1940), 332 pp. In this autobiography by
    the articulate Cornell-educated wife of Stanford's first
    registrar, Elliott proves to be a keen and outspoken ob-
    server of early campus life.

Elliott, Orrin Leslie, *Stanford University: The First Twenty-Five
    Years* (Stanford: Stanford University Press, 1937), 624 pp.
    Detailed and reliable account of the university's first
    years, its founding, philosophy, and culture, as well as of
    student life and key events, by Stanford's first registrar
    and close friend and colleague of the first president.

English Club, *First Year at Stanford: A Sketch of Pioneer Days at
    Leland Stanford Junior University* (Stanford: English Club,
    1905), 159 pp. Pioneer alumni and faculty recount life at
    the infant, isolated campus community of the early
    1890's.

Jordan, David Starr, *The Days of a Man: Being Memories of a
    Naturalist, Teacher and Minor Prophet of Democracy* (New
    York: World Book Company, 1922), 2 vols., 906 pp. This
    autobiography of Stanford's charismatic and gregarious
    first president describes his life in higher education, sci-
    ence, and American reform movements of the late nine-
    teenth and early twentieth centuries.

Korff, J. Michael, *Student Control and University Government at
    Stanford: The Evolving Student-University Relationship* (un-

published Ph.D. dissertation, Stanford University, 1975), 246 pp. Based on extensive research in the university's archives, this study of the relationship between the student body and the faculty and administration also reveals much about the backgrounds, values, and viewpoints of Stanford students.

Liebendorfer, Don E., *The Color of Life Is Red: A History of Stanford Athletics, 1892–1972* (Stanford: Dept. of Athletics, Stanford University, 1972), 132 pp. Basic history of major intercollegiate men's sports at Stanford.

McDonald, Emanuel B., *Sam McDonald's Farm* (Stanford: Stanford University Press, 1954), 422 pp. Lengthy autobiography by Stanford's superintendent of athletic grounds and buildings and close friend and advisor to generations of Stanford students.

Mirrielees, Edith, ed., *Stanford Mosaic: Reminiscences of the First Seventy-Five Years at Stanford University* (Stanford: Stanford University Press, 1962), 248 pp. Brief, evocative recollections by alumni from the pioneer years to the early 1960's.

Mirrielees, Edith, *Stanford: The Story of a University* (New York: G. P. Putnam's Sons, 1959), 255 pp. This entertaining history of the university by an alumna ('07) and popular English professor is based on long personal acquaintance with the campus as well as on historical accounts— unfortunately for the historian, at times it is difficult to tell which.

Mitchell, J. Pearce, *Stanford University, 1916–1941* (Stanford: Stanford University Press, 1958), 167 pp. Mitchell followed Elliott as the right-hand man to the president as well as university chronicler. His history of the Wilbur years reflects the era's interest in administrative and curricular reform, increased administrative involvement in student life, and campus growth.

Nash, George, *Herbert Hoover and Stanford University* (Stanford: Hoover Institution Press, 1988), 241 pp. Much of Stanford's administrative development is revealed in the story of Hoover's growth from outgoing undergraduate to anonymous donor to highly influential trustee. Hoover's contributions to and impact on the campus are meticulously documented.

Stanford Alumni Association, *Stanford Alumnus*, 1899–1917; *Stanford Illustrated Review*, 1916–1940; *Stanford Alumni Review*, 1940–1951. The Alumni Association's monthly magazine changed names several times but continued to report campus news ranging from administrative changes to athletics, new facilities to curriculum issues, faculty research to student life. Along with the *Stanford Daily* (until 1927 named the *Daily Palo Alto*), which has been in continuous operation since 1892, these periodicals are a rich and essential resource on campus life.

Stanford University, *Report of the President*, 1903–1948. A chronicle of accomplishments and changes on both a university-wide and department level, the yearly reports submitted by university officers and department heads provide a useful summary from the administration's eyes of faculty research, administrative concerns, student affairs, curriculum issues, and development trends.

Stanford University: The Founding Grant, with Amendments, Legislation and Court Decrees (Stanford: Stanford University, 1987). The essential legal documents regarding the founding of the university and its later development, including amendments to the grant by Jane Stanford and legislation affecting the University.

Turner, Paul V., Marcia E. Vetrocq, and Karen Weitze, *The Founders and the Architects: The Design of Stanford University* (Stanford: Dept. of Art, Stanford University, 1976), 96 pp. Key study of the relationship between Jane and Leland Stanford and the men employed to design a memorial to their son, and of the resulting campus design. Well documented, with a wealth of photographs, drawings, and maps.

Wilbur, Ray Lyman, *The Memoirs of Ray Lyman Wilbur, 1875–1949.* (Stanford: Stanford University Press, 1960), 687 pp. An alumnus of the class of 1896, in his career as physician, dean, and university president, Wilbur never strayed far from Stanford. His autobiography portrays Stanford's growth from the perspective of a powerful administrator.

THE STANFORD FAMILY

The professional and personal papers of the Stanford family, preserved in the Stanford University Archives, include correspondence, interviews and news articles, documents, photographs, monographs, and journal articles about the family and their many business and philanthropic interests. In addition, the following titles provide background about Leland Stanford, Jane Lathrop Stanford, and Leland Stanford Jr. essential to the study of their roles in creating and building Stanford University and to the development of the broader concept of a "Stanford family" of alumni, faculty, and staff.

Berner, Bertha, *Mrs. Leland Stanford: An Intimate Account* (Stanford: Stanford University Press, 1935), 231 pp. This very personal and sentimental account of life with Mrs. Stanford from 1885 to 1905 by her devoted companion and secretary provides rare insight into Stanford family life.

Clark, George T., *Leland Stanford: War Governor of California, Railroad Builder, and Founder of Stanford University* (Stanford: Stanford University Press, 1931), 491 pp. This first sympathetic biography of Stanford based on both documentation and extensive interviews resulted in the preservation of additional family papers. Especially valuable is the final chapter, "Building a University," in which Leland Stanford's plans throughout 1884–91 are painstakingly documented.

Mozley, Anita, et al., *Eadweard Muybridge: The Stanford Years* (Stanford: Dept. of Art, Stanford University, 1972), 136 pp. This extensive exhibition catalog documents the horse-in-motion experiments at the Palo Alto Farm and the very different talents and intentions of Muybridge the photographer and Stanford the businessman. An excellent and definitive study of their contributions.

Nagel, Gunther, *Iron Will: The Life and Letters of Jane Lathrop Stanford*, 2nd ed. (Stanford: Stanford Alumni Association, 1985), 224 pp. As yet the only biography of Jane Stanford, this work evolved from the story told in Mrs. Stanford's correspondence. Though a sentimental account, it offers Mrs. Stanford's views and experiences in her own words.

Osborne, Carol, *Museum Builders in the West: The Stanfords as Collectors and Patrons of Art, 1870–1906* (Stanford: Stanford University Museum of Art, 1986), 139 pp. This well-written and thoughtful study of Jane and Leland Stanford as art patrons and collectors places the establishment of the university and Jane Stanford's continued interest in the development of the museum in the larger context of the Stanfords' lives and interests. It also provides a balanced view of Leland Stanford Jr.'s interests and talents, and his contributions to his parents' interests in art, archaeology, and education.

Stanford, Jane. *Addresses to the Leland Stanford Junior University Board of Trustees, 1897–1903* (Stanford: Stanford University, 1897–1903; reprinted in *Stanford University: The Founding Grant*, Stanford University, 1987). As surviving founder after Leland Stanford's death in 1893, Jane Stanford wielded enormous influence on the development of the university for another decade. Her addresses, serving as amendments to the Founding Grant, clarified the founders' intents and in some cases changed the course of university history.

Stanford, Leland, *'Speech to the Board of Trustees,' 1885, and 'Opening Day Address,' 1891* (Stanford: Stanford University, 1891). Leland Stanford left no autobiographical writings, but two major sources regarding his educational philosophy remain: written accounts from interviews with the news media and, later, university personnel and these two widely circulated addresses.

Tutorow, Norman, *Leland Stanford: Man of Many Careers* (Menlo Park: Pacific Coast Publishers, 1971), 317 pp. Seeking to present a broader portrait than that of railroad baron and politician, Tutorow describes a life of many careers including that of the California wine grower ahead of his time and of innovative horse breeder and trainer. This biography counters the more superficial portraits presented by Hubert Howe Bancroft (*History of the Life of Leland Stanford*, 1952) and Oscar Lewis (*The Big Four*, 1938) but avoids critical analysis of the impact of Stanford's Southern Pacific Company on western American development or power struggles with Central Pacific Railroad associates.

NEWS SERVICE PUBLICATIONS

Two excellent historical publications are available from the university News Service:

Bartholomew, Karen. *The Design of a University* (special section, *Stanford Observer*, April 1987), 12 pp.

Bartholomew, Karen, and Roxanne Nilan. *Stanford: A Centennial Chronology* (special edition, *Stanford Observer*, April 1987), 32 pp. with index.

Index

299

The Stanford Album is published by Stanford University Press in honor
of the centennial of the founding of the Leland Stanford Junior University.

Designed by Anita Walker Scott

Composed by Wilsted & Taylor, Oakland, California, in Linotron Palatino

Printed by Meriden-Stinehour Press, Lunenburg, Vermont, on acid-free paper

Bound by Acme Bookbinding, Charlestown, Massachusetts

PHOTOGRAPHIC CREDITS

We are grateful to the individuals and institutions who gave us per-
mission to reproduce their photographs in this book, as listed here.
All other photographs are from the collections of the Stanford University Archives. (Abbreviations: t, top; c, center; b, bottom; l, left;
r, right)

3 (tl, tr), Stanford University Museum of Art; 6 (tl), Jim Ludlam; 6
(cl), Bobbe Harris Brock; 6 (br), Mary Lou Andreatta Zeppenfeld; 7
(t), Jeannette Hill McCarty; 7 (b), Tro Harper; 18 (tr, cr), Palo Alto
Historical Association; 27 (tl), Stanford University Museum of Art;
36 (t, c), Stanford University News Service; 38, Stanford University
Museum of Art; 114 (tr), Hoover Institution Archives; 124 (t), Lane
Medical Archives; 131 (tl), Linda Atkinson; 149 (br), Stanford University News Service; 170 (tl, b), 171, Hoover Institution Archives;
184 (tr, tl), Stanford University News Service; 206–7, Stanford University School of Earth Sciences; 210 (b), Hoover Institution Archives; 212 (t, b), 213 (t, b), Lane Medical Archives; 214 (t), Hoover
Institution Archives; 218, Jeannette Hill McCarty; 220, Tro Harper;
222 (b), Jim Ludlam; 227 (tl), Tro Harper; 227 (tr), Jim Ludlam; 227
(b), Tro Harper; 229 (t), Jim Ludlam; 229 (br), Jeannette Gould
Maino; 230 (cl), Charles Dalliba Marple, M.D.; 230 (tr), Stanley A.
Rosin; 230 (cr), Ira "Red" Cross; 233 (tl), Ronald S. Callvert; 523 (tr),
J. P. Cahn; 233 (c), Tro Harper; 234 (tl), Roger H. White; 234 (tr), Jo-
seph H. Davis, M.D.; 240, Jeannette Hill McCarty; 241 (tl), Dick
Spencer; 241 (cl), Jeannette Hill McCarty; 241 (bl), Caroline Had-
dock Reuland; 241 (tr), Jim Ludlam; 241 (br), Jeannette Hill Mc-

Carty; 243 (tr), David L. Crandall; 245 (tr), Richards Lyon; 248 (b),
Tro Harper; 251 (bl, br), Jim Ludlam; 252–53, 254, Roger H. White;
255 (tl), John W. Bustard; 255 (tr, b), Roger H. White; 256, Stanford
University School of Earth Sciences; 259 (tr), Lane Medical Archives;
259 (br), 260 (t), 261 (t, c, b), 263 (b), Tro Harper; 267 (t), Lois Williams Rosebrook; 267 (b), Mary Lou Andreatta Zeppenfeld; 268, Bill
Hyer; 269 (t, c, b), Lois Williams Rosebrook; 270, Bill Hyer; 271 (t),
Roger H. White; 275 (tl, tr), Judy Wood Shrader; 277 (tl, bl), Mary
Lou Andreatta Zeppenfeld; 279 (t), Stanford University News Service; 279 (b), Mr. and Mrs. Frank W. Hodgden III; 280 (tl, tr), Ann
Beyer Wert; 280 (bl), Dana Fore Eggleston; 281 (tl), Lois Williams Rosebrook; 281 (bl), Dana Fore Eggleston; 281 (tr), Mary Lou Andreatta Zeppenfeld; 284 (t), Margaret W. Tuttle; 284 (b), David L.
Crandall; 286 (l, r), Bill Hyer; 287 (tr), Lois Williams Rosebrook; 287
(l), Tro Harper; 287 (br), 288 (t), Mary Lou Andreatta Zeppenfeld;
288 (c), Lois Williams Rosebrook; 290 (tl), Stanford University News
Service

Library of Congress Cataloging-in-Publication Data

Davis, Margo Baumgartner.
    The Stanford album: a photographic history, 1885–1945
    Margo Davis, Roxanne Nilan.
    p.   cm.
Bibliography: p.   Includes index.   ISBN 0-8047-1639-0 (alk. paper)
1. Stanford University—History.   2. Stanford University—Description—Views.
I. Nilan, Roxanne.   II. Title.   89-4500
LD3028.D38   1989   378.794′73—dc20   CIP